THE SOVIET EXPERIMENT

BY THE SAME AUTHOR

*A Compilation of the Laws Relating to Corrupt Practices
at Elections in the United States*

†

Judicial Decisions Affecting the Corrupt Practices Laws

†

Crime and the Criminal Law in the United States

†

*The Deaf: Their Position in Society and the Provision
for Their Education in the United States*

†

*The Blind: Their Condition and the Work Being Done
for Them in the United States*

†

Blindness and the Blind in the United States

†

Deafness and the Deaf in the United States (forthcoming)

THE
SOVIET EXPERIMENT.

BY

HARRY BEST

Professor of Sociology, University of Kentucky;
Formerly of the University Settlement, New York

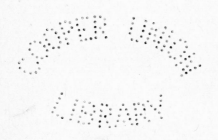

RICHARD R. SMITH • 1941
NEW YORK

COPYRIGHT 1941 BY RICHARD R. SMITH
120 EAST 39TH STREET, NEW YORK, N. Y.

SET UP BY BROWN BROTHERS LINOTYPERS
PRINTED IN THE UNITED STATES OF AMERICA
BY THE FERRIS PRINTING COMPANY

PREFACE

Despite all that has been written regarding Soviet Russia, there is believed to be need for a relatively brief account that will enable alike the man in the street and the college student to obtain a wider and clearer understanding of what has happened there. The present work has been prepared, not so much with the intent of presenting something new regarding the movements in that land, but rather as a study of the social philosophy underlying what has taken place. It is based upon three sources: (1) rather extensive reading upon the subject; (2) conversations with persons holding different points of view who have been to Russia; and (3) personal observations made when the writer had the privilege of visiting Russia at one time "on his own," without membership in official parties and without official guidance (except when especially requested).

CONTENTS

EXTENT AND RESOURCES OF SOVIET RUSSIA

Russia, or what was known as Russia, still remains in consequence of its "Revolution" a land of uncertainty. It is here that has taken place what in the range of its operations has hardly been surpassed among the startling events of history. For in that process there has been a change in that spacious country from one of the most autocratic and least democratic lands of all time to a land under an absolutism no less real, but a dictatorship representing the proletariat of the country, a dictatorship presumed to be in the hands of the workers and peasants. Under it there has been transpiring a vast experiment, involving not only the accustomed economic principles and bases of the production and distribution of wealth, but the adoption of a new social philosophy, a new manner of life, a new civilization, all different from what the world has hitherto accepted. The things that have been made use of by man in the past, some of them venerated, have been overturned, or thrust aside, or crushed under foot, to make way for another order.

In Soviet Russia is embraced a far-reaching area—in fact, one-sixth of the area of the entire earth. It is a territory exceeded only by that of the globe-encircling elements of the British Empire. It takes in almost all of the eastern half of Europe, and northern and much of central Asia. It stretches from polar regions to sub-tropical regions.

This vast land is as yet quite underpopulated, but it is potentially capable of containing several teeming billions. Russia is no longer the official name of a country and will not be as long as the country is in the hands of its present rulers. What was once known as Russia is embraced in the Union of Socialist Soviet Republics (U.S.S.R.). This may have annexed to it and united with it any region in the world subscribing to its political and economic formula; the name of the whole remains unchanged.

The U.S.S.R. is composed of a conglomeration of almost two hundred different races and nationalities. Embraced within its wide bounds is a descending scale of areas, territories, or groups—union republics, autonomous republics, autonomous provinces, autonomous areas, besides undesignated regions. There is in all a population of some one hundred and seventy million (perhaps increased by over twenty million with the addition of new territories).

Not all of old Russia, nor "all the Russias" (as the former Czars used to call it), has been under the Soviet government. All the nationalities to the west were sloughed off for a time, taking advantage of troubled conditions when the Czar's government suffered collapse—Poland, Lithuania, Latvia, Estonia, Finland. Towards the east, in Asia, however, U.S.S.R. has had hold of practically all of the farthest reaches of the former Empire, including some doubtful or disputed territory.

It is, however, those who are known and will continue to be known as Russians—Russian Slavs—who constitute much the larger proportion—approximately three-fourths —of the population of the Union. It is to be remembered that the Russians are themselves divided into three distinct groups: the Great Russians, who center about Moscow (the Muscovites), constituting about one-half of the entire population; the Little Russians, who inhabit southern Russia and front upon the Black Sea (the Ukrainians), numbering about one-fifth; and the White Russians, who live in southwest Russia and are nearest to western Europe, amounting to about three per cent. There is another Slavic group in Soviet Russia, though not identified with the Russians proper—a considerable group of Poles who had become separated from their fellow countrymen in what was Poland.

Smaller proportions are of various nationalities. The largest proportions of non-Slavic elements, with about two per cent each, are Uzbecks, Tartars, and Jews (mostly in White Russia). Other smaller groups, usually concentrated in some section, are Germans, Finns, Turks, Caucasians, Georgians, Armenians, Greeks, Persians, etc. Spreading across Asia is a heterogeneous mass.

Projecting farthest into Europe are the Slavs, together with less extensive clusters of other whites (including those who inhabit the historic Caucasus regions). Lying in eastern Europe and western Asia are peoples who are largely Turco-Tartar, finally shading off into Mongolians in farthest Asia. Some groups in the latter Continent are hardly more than nomadic tribes. In all the Soviet land are something like one hundred and fifty languages and dialects.

U.S.S.R. is a territory of great wealth so far as natural resources are concerned—in not a few respects being second to no other country on the globe, and being nearly self-sufficient. In many parts the soil is very rich. Natural resources are abundant and varied, with nearly all elements known to man. In timber the country comes first, having nearly three-tenths of the world's present reserves. It contains the richest deposits of manganese in the world. It is foremost in stores of potassium, platinum, and even gold. The country has almost measureless sources of potential wealth such as oil and coal and iron. Copper, zinc, lead, phosphates, and peat abound. All kinds of stones, including precious stones are possessed. Other mineral deposits are of wide variety and in large quantities. The extent of water power can not easily be computed.

Further forms of wealth does Soviet Russia have. It constitutes one of the granaries of the earth. It produces about three-fifths of the rye of the world, one-fifth of the barley and oats, and one-fifth of the wheat. Other agricultural products range from cotton and tobacco and tea and sugar to flax and hemp and silk. Of the development of the fur industry only a beginning has been made. The same is true of the fishing industry. A great future is possible for such industries as the production of live stock, fruit, eggs.

The Russian people are themselves of a kind to win men's affection. They are simple, honest, generous, warm-hearted, patient, long-suffering, of high imaginative powers, passive, non-resistant—at times perhaps passionate, perhaps quick in headstrong action or in despair.

They have been a people living in the sixteenth century. With them religion soon has passed into superstition; regard for their ruler, into a lively worship of their Little Father. From oppression and crushing misrule they have suffered for ages; in their faces has been written the long, long years of suffering.

The Russian people are a semi-Asiatic people, standing on the edge of Europe, and during most of their history with their faces turned to the east rather than to the west. They have been slow finding their destinies with the people of Europe. They have looked upon the people of Europe somewhat as strangers. In the days of Peter the Great and Catherine the Great certain attempts were made to westernize Russia, culminating in the founding of St.

Petersburg, which could have a window upon Europe. Here were put on, at least in court circles, the airs of western Europe. But the Russian people would have none of it. St. Petersburg remained an upstart city, away from the life of the people. In their hearts it was holy mother Moscow that had their affection. Western Europe to them remained far off.

And Russia knows the peoples of the east, even when they have come as foes. Standing on the hills overlooking Moscow from the west, one can easily look beyond the gleaming, white-walled city, with its glistening, golden towers and pinnacles—a very dream of beauty and romance, not greatly impaired by modern structures—and without great effort of the imagination glimpse the illimitable plains sweeping ever and ever on into the vast east, till they are finally lapped by the waters of the Pacific. One still can behold the hosts of Tartars and of Mongols on horseback, sweeping west from that boundless east, hungry for the treasures of the Muscovites.

CHAPTER II

ECONOMIC ANTECEDENTS OF THE SOVIET REVOLUTION

I N THE change of Russia from its Czaristic days to those of the Soviet power, there have been two forces or movements converging each upon the other, and preordained to meet in the fullness of time. One was the radical or revolutionary movement, creeping over a greater and greater part of Europe, and not entirely slighting Russia —a movement having existed under ground in Europe for over a century, and now taking organized shape as communism. The other movement was that of the strange, vast Czaristic empire slowly tottering to its dissolution.

In a fashion the revolution in Russia can trace descent from the French revolution of the latter days of the eighteenth century, or at least from the thoughts loosened by that revolution—furthered by the rapid developments consequent upon the so-called industrial revolution, especially in the use of steam power and in the concentration of man in factories for the making of things to supply human wants. Following thereupon were various proposals for a new order in the production and distribution of wealth among men. In France, in particular, there was a whole line of projects offered, some of highly fantastic nature— by Babeuf, St. Simon, Cabet, Proudhon, Blanc, Fourier. With the passage of time, however, in most of the countries of Europe the proposals generally became more conservative or of more practical character; they were rather measures of social reform, and for the most part not of a particularly radical cast. Aims were chiefly greater participation in government by the working classes, extension of the franchise to male adults generally, improved labor conditions, reduction of privileges for the few, wider education, more equitable schemes of taxation, more humane criminal codes, and similar measures of social and economic betterment. The one outstanding, telling document that appeared in the nineteenth century was the Communist Manifesto, a blast prepared by an international group (1848). This document was of pretty radical and almost violent character; it was harsh, materialistic, somewhat unfair—but withal a thought-provoking thing. It was a fiery indictment of a capitalistic society, and included its stirring appeal to the working classes of the world to unite, who had "nothing to lose but their chains," and "a world to gain."

The adoption of any measures of reform during this period faced a stone wall. Though a large part of what was then demanded (apart from the Communist Manifesto) now receives general assent, the proposals at the time incurred deep opposition from the ruling powers; and in more than one country there was an abortive revolution—a repercussion of which was the migration of some excellent citizens from Europe to a more liberal America.

The time was now ripe for the entry upon the scene of one of the great figures of all history, a man comparable to Mohammed for his success in building a following of uncountable numbers who accept without question his deliverances—a man whose thought still holds dominion over a large part of the world. This was Karl Marx, the great German scholarly socialist. It was he who had a large part in the writing of the Communist Manifesto. It is to be said, however, that others at this time, especially Engel, Rodbertus and La Salle, had much to do with the movement now set on foot; even philosophers like Kant,

Hegel, and Fichte are to be credited with having furnished some of its basic conceptions.

Marx aimed at more direct procedure—a direct appeal to the working classes of the countries of Europe, and indeed of all the world. He sought to show them how they had been exploited, and would continue to be exploited, till they themselves took possession of the machinery of capitalism. His great philosophy of life—for it is nothing less—centers about and is built upon the material forces (in particular, food, raiment, and shelter) upon which man has to count for his living. These become the only forces to be reckoned with in man's social life, or indeed in his civilization. It is this "economic interpretation of history" which is Marx's starting point. Man's struggle for tools for the production of things for his needs is the primary and underlying struggle of human existence. The class struggle is the struggle between the owners of these tools (the capitalist class) and those who are not owners but are compelled to work for the owners (the proletarian class). The bourgeoisie class, mostly small traders and groups owning little capital themselves, but dependent upon the capitalist class, are really allies of it. The working class, beaten so far in the conflict, have to accept wages from the capitalist class for the labor they do, their physical labor being all they have to give in return for means of living. They have thus the status of wage slaves. The wealth created beyond what is returned to the workers as wages is surplus value, which is entirely unearned on the part of the capitalist class. The profit, interest, and rent which are received in society are unfair, and come really from the despoiling of the worker. Under these circumstances the condition of the working class goes from worse to worse, their misery increases, till finally, goaded beyond all endurance, they rise up and seize possession of the tools of the capitalist class. As the capitalist class knows no country, but extends its operations everywhere, so the working class will do likewise; theirs will become an international movement. A powerful class consciousness will grip the workers of all nations; together they will march to victory. In extreme Marxian thought, finally, when socialism is in complete mastery of the field, there will be no need of the agencies of government, but only coöperative groups among citizens; there will be a classless society, in an order of abundance; and the state will "wither away."

Not only this, but the "morality," the "civilization" of capitalist countries is based upon capitalistic principles, and reflects capitalistic attitudes. Accepted standards of civilization are thus wrong from top to bottom. No individual is to blame—socialism never becomes personal—but the system is altogether bad; and it is the system which must be destroyed.

It was this doctrine of Marx which swept over great areas of Europe, and has held so vast a sway. It is classical, orthodox, Marxian socialism.

Most of Europe, especially central and northern Europe, concerned with radical economic reform, followed Marx, but with an increasing measure of conservatism. There was little faith in revolution, as this was believed to be a real detriment to the cause; activities were more and more confined to an appeal to the suffrage. Even the theories of Marx have undergone a process of toning down. Under Bernstein in Germany, in particular, with his "revisionist" policy, the Marxian philosophy had become less dogmatic and more opportunist. Some of the leading postulates, especially that of the increasing misery of the working classes under the capitalistic system, were seen to be fallacies, at variance with the unfolding facts of human experience.

Thus have developed some of the so-called socialistic

parties of Europe, often called by some such name as social democratic, which can be denominated as only partly socialistic. They have generally been "right wing" groups. Their programs are not very "red" after all; hardly enough, in fact, to cause dismay among fairly conservative people. They have been engaged in a mighty battle against "left wing" groups, which are decidedly radical and revolutionary. The combat between these groups has raged vehemently and has often been more bitter than any combat between them and other groups.

For the revolutionary groups of Europe the orderly processes of socialism would not do. They were not thorough enough. The kingdom was to be taken by violence. Developments here have resulted in the more extreme variety of modern communism in Europe. The newer system may be said to have had its formal beginning in 1863 in London. (It was in England that such movements could be started without police interference). There was formed what was called the International Workingmen's Association, or the first "International." After a few years a second International was created, only to fall to pieces at the outbreak of the World War. In 1923 it was renewed, with comparatively moderate tendencies. (In 1871 there was in Paris, France, just after the Franco-German war, a brief but sanguinary experiment under what has been known as the Paris Commune.)

It was to some extent from the first International that organized radical communism may be said to have its origin—for it emphasizes the international aspects of the movement even more than does the more sober brand of socialism. Though at the beginning of rather confused character, without an altogether definite or positive program, and in some respects on the way toward anarchism, it was able to secure a certain following in some countries, especially in southern Europe, and to a slight extent in

Russia. This movement was of openly destructive character, the torch or the bomb being a recognized instrument of its procedure. Much of its virulence was directed towards the crowned heads and ministers of state. The movement did not confine its operations to the economic readjustment of society, though its operations were declared to spring from this motive. It was not only prepared to attack capitalism, but it may be said to have declared for a wider emancipation: from the state, from religion, and perhaps to some extent from strict marriage ties. (Towards these things Marxian socialism is supposed to have some very liberal views; but in general under it these matters are taken as purely personal ones, and not within its prerogatives.) Under the more violent communism or under anarchism, as then proclaimed, all these things were believed to interfere with the freedom of the individual, and at least to some extent to buttress hated capitalism. So far as there has been a difference between communism and socialism, the one is much more intolerant than the other, and asserts itself in much more dogmatic terms. Communism is the more likely to regard force as a rightful weapon for the attainment of its ends. It can more easily pass into despotism.

Whether looked upon in connection with the movement in Russia or not, communism has stood forth as one of the great, overshadowing problems with which modern society has had to deal. Apart from totalitarianism in other forms, it has, in its momentousness, been second to only one other thing—war. In more than one country of Europe it has been the outstanding, the primary problem. Extra police vigilance and preparation for certain days of the year or mysterious watch fires on some mountain top have been sufficient attestations of the gravity of the situation. Communism appeals with particular force to the most ignorant, the most discouraged, the most wretched, the most des-

perate, and those with the least to lose among the masses
of men. It can well be compared to cancer in the physical
body. Neither is well understood, and adequate measures
for dealing with neither have yet arrived; but greater
progress is doubtless being made with respect to physical
cancer than with respect to communism. Communism is
indicative of unrest and threatened revolt—that all is not
well in the nether regions of society. Humankind, with
all its learning and skill and ingenuity, has seemed quite
unable to find a complete cure. Its continued presence
constitutes an indictment against our civilization.

Communists, with their radical political, economic, and
social program, abide the time when they can proceed to
put their program into practice. They may use peaceable
means to obtain their objectives; if such are not at hand,
resort may be had to violence, or to the use of physical
force. Communists may be said to be constantly lying in
wait for such dissatisfaction or disturbance, especially of
an industrial nature, as will sweep them into their desired
power. They stand ready to play upon industrial disputes,
to seize upon and exploit troubled industrial situations.
They exaggerate evil living or working conditions—bad
as they may already be. They fan whatever flames of
industrial discontent they can discover, adding fuel to the
spreading flames. They sow seeds of discord and dissen-
sion in the industrial life of a people. They encourage,
foment, and provoke clashes with the police or with those
charged with the keeping of order and the peace, berating
and denouncing officers of the law, and seeking to awaken
hostility towards existing government. If necessary, they
are prepared to take a more decided, more active stand.
All the while they declare themselves the one retreat and
refuge of the underpaid and overworked in human society,
of the oppressed and dispossessed; and point to the happy
haven to be reached when power is entrusted to them.

The various tactics employed are to redound to their bene-fit and advantage. To the communists the world is a mission field.

Communism, as was to be expected, had hardly started upon its way when it began to clash with government, in particular with the officials of government. Its leaders, at times men of force and education, were hunted from place to place, much as outlaws, and had to spend most of their time in hiding. But the fires of the movement, smoldering though they were, were kept alive, and were ready to burst into flame at the opportune moment. No movement ever appeared at so propitious a time as did communism at the time of the collapse of the Russian empire. In the later years of the World War another inter-national, called the Third International, was organized in Switzerland; and on the achievement of the revolution in Russia the headquarters were moved to that country. Moscow now remains in principle the center for an upris-ing of the workers of all nations, and for the adoption of communism everywhere.

CHAPTER III

THE BREAKDOWN OF THE CZARISTIC REGIME

THE second great event responsible for what has happened in Russia was the approaching dissolution of the Russian Empire, an institution sooner or later doomed through its own inherent weakness to perish under the conditions of modern civilization. When men come to think of it, they may well wonder that such an autocracy as that in control of Czaristic Russia, essentially Asiatic in character, could have been projected into Europe and could have remained so long side by side with western civilization. That government had for long been hardly less than a blot upon human civilization. Russia, while ostensibly a European nation, and in actual alliance with some of the advanced peoples of Europe, was little more than an Oriental despotism with a thin veneer of European efficiency and culture. Not many of its rulers, with the exception of Peter the Great and Catherine the Great, were strong or commanding personalities, or really capable of leading a great people. With a few glowing exceptions, the nobility, often dissolute and dissipated, was a heavy burden and trial to the Russian people. It contained probably the grandest gang of gamblers in Europe. It was almost entirely wanting in any sense of obligation to better the life of the common people. The attitude of the Russian autocracy in general was one of incomprehension and stupidity; when it moved, its action was usually one of arbitrary caprice or brutish force. Most of the Czars had themselves had peculiarly sad lives: their golden crowns usually carried tragedy with them. Ever since the diadem was placed upon the brow of the first of the Romanoffs, some dread disaster had pursued the imperial family. Life with them had been insecure and uncertain, despite legions of troops for the protection of the Little Father. Probably there have been few really happy days spent by the Czars of Russia.

Conditions in Russia during the years preceding the World War were indeed truly deplorable. A large part of the population lived in wretchedness and in hopelessness. Many of the peasants were on the verge of starvation most of the year. Serfdom had been abolished only half a century before; but, despite its formal end, rent laws and regulations were still keenly oppressive, and the liberation of those who tilled the soil did not proceed far. Few of the landlords were themselves to be called well off, and there was little capital available for needed improvements. The limited industrial undertakings in the larger cities were for the most part in a backward state. It was even charged that a peasantry in that state was preferred by the rulers, because of their fear of an industrial nation. Barren alike were rural and urban life. Social welfare measures for the great body of the population hardly existed on any considerable scale. Legislation in the interests of the working classes had made little progress. The death rate was among the highest in the world. Cultural opportunities, especially in the way of education, were meagre and poor; to a considerable part of the population they were practically denied. Formal religion was to no small extent superstition; to no small extent it was intolerant. Government was inefficient, and at times rotten to the core. Corruption grew in high places and in low. Bureaucracy was overdeveloped; when honest it might be slow or arrogant. For offenders against the law, not a few of whom were political offenders, punishment was often barbarous: the world knows the story of the long lines wending their heavy way to Siberia. Russia was a land filled with unhappy, miserable human beings: it was there that man was brother to the ox.

Nor did matters improve with time. Those who ruled Russia could not or would not see. National and language groups were ruthlessly ground under foot. If there appeared a glimmer of relief or surcease from oppression, it was followed by reaction and renewed severities. If promises were secured from the government, they turned out for the most part to be meaningless. In 1905, under the chastening defeat by Japan, there was hope in the hearts of many that the time had arrived for the remedying of the most intolerable abuses. A constitution, such as it was, was proclaimed; and a duma, or parliamentary assembly, was created, supposedly to take the place of the old bureaucratic régime. The duma, while a genuine step forward, was not fully representative; it did not have its roots deep in the land. Whatever redress was obtained was not great. Reform did not go far.

Down to the time of the revolution the Czar's government pursued its despotic, cruel way, refusing to hear the cries from its subjects or to offer any wide program for the amelioration of their condition. Reasonable demands of the duma were nearly always rejected; those that were granted were yielded reluctantly. Leaders who were moderate in their proposals and who were as much opposed to revolution as were the Czar's counsellors usually met only rebuff or worse for their pains.

During all these preliminary days, there was no possibility of there being built up a great middle class—between the few educated and the illiterate masses—fitted for self-government, or fitted for the construction of an orderly, progressive democracy. In the large cities, where opportunities were greater for discussion of public questions, and where liberal but not radical doctrines could have had a hearing, already revolutionary propaganda was at work. Virtually the only persons who could under-stand the situation and could take a helpful part in it were the students and professors in the universities, and these largely as a result of contacts with western Europe. Nearly all these demanded certain liberties and the reform of various abuses; some became undisguised or qualified socialists.

Long before the revolution discontent and unrest had been growing steadily. In later days protests and uprisings became more numerous and more open. These were in the main of local and isolated character, but some had sanguinary accompaniments. The severe punishment meted out only added to the gloom of the land. Russia in time became filled with those waiting their day of venge-ance.

The movements in western Europe, relatively conserva-tive in character as they were, were passing Russia by. The very fact that Russia was off to itself made it the possible prey of fiery revolutions. It was in Russia only that such a curious force as nihilism—empty, incoherent, shapeless thing that it was—could have life. It was some-thing driven up from the darkness and oppression of the land. It was below anarchism even, and represented only the blackness of terror and despair.

In the event of a political upheaval in Russia it was the extreme or left wing element of the radical movement that would mount the saddle, and would have no more regard for moderate socialism than for downright capitalism. In it would be embraced in greater or less measure the revolutionary conceptions as to the state and as to capi-talism, and also as to religion and the family. It would attempt to set up a new social order, a new civilization, based upon a philosophy different from anything the world had before tried.

CHAPTER IV

FORCES LOOSENED IN THE WORLD WAR

WHEN the World War started, radicalism was not at the fore in Russia, no matter to what extent it was smoldering under the surface. So patriotic were the Russian people that they were quite ready to forget their own ills. They were eager to befriend and protect their fellow Slavs in Europe. At the front the Russian soldier was brave, and gave his life without complaint. Perhaps he had inferior weapons or no weapons; even with weapons he could not count upon the quality of his ammunition supply if indeed he had any. He had at times to fight with a club or with his bare hands—perhaps he had to wait till a comrade by his side had fallen, and then seize the released weapon and fight on. Besides the enemy at his front, there was a persistent enemy at his rear—hunger; and in addition, lack of hospital equipment and all else that goes with war to rob it of some of its horrors. There were also incompetence, graft, corruption. Russia, with all its array of soldiers, was in war clumsy and slow-moving; it was unprepared for war. Not enough producers were left behind on the land; transportation facilities were grossly inadequate; losses in battle were frightful. Disillusionment and demoralization could not be far away. The whole military system of Russia, along with its government, was on the verge of crashing down.

The Russian soldier, weary and hungry, not understanding why he was still fighting, was now ready to listen to any program that would promise him surcease from his misery. It was the revolutionary party, always active in subterranean channels, and long biding its time, that came with soft whisperings in his ear. It was through the use of four magic words that the Soviet party won his adhesion—peace, liberty, food, land. He might comprehend little of the high-sounding and intricate phrases of communism, but he did know what these magic words meant. He knew what peace meant, because he had gone through months of bitter war, with untold suffering, and amid heaps of dead men's bodies. He knew what food meant, for during most of that period he was not far from starvation. He knew what liberty meant, for all his life he had seen only the heavy yoke of oppression. He knew what land meant, for this he had craved from his earliest days. When the Soviet party had won over the soldiers and the army, their *coup d'état* was complete.

It is not to be thought that there was a real revolution in Russia, in the sense that there occurred a heavy clash of armed forces, with resulting assumption of power by the victorious side. The matter was not so simple as that, or perhaps was simpler. The Soviet party or the Bolsheviki did not seize power. Such action was not necessary. It was ripe to their hands, or to the hands of any organized group with any following who could pick it up. Though once recognized as one of the mighty empires of the world, and protected by myriads of soldiery, the Czaristic government was builded upon the frailest of foundations; beneath it was no enlightened democracy or popular will, or even popular understanding. When the storm broke upon it, as it was in time bound to do, there was nothing whatever to stay its collapse. In those days of 1917 order literally faded away; it disappeared. There was none to carry on government. True, there were the groups headed by Kerensky and Miliukov and others of moderate tendencies; but these were small, and there was no actual following for them. Whatever exercise of power was attempted by the provisional government after the abdication of the Czar had an early end.

CHAPTER V

ASSUMPTION OF POWER BY THE SOVIET

IT WAS into this breach that the Soviet party stepped. It had one thing which no other party had—a program. It knew what it wanted. It was remarkably well organized. It had some highly skilled and able leaders: some were little short of geniuses at organization. It was schooled through hard Czaristic experiences. Its membership was small—only a handful of city workers, representing a very limited section of the Russian population. But it was equal to the occasion. Not often in history has there been at a time of crisis a group so cool, so resourceful, so determined, and so entirely prepared to assume the mastery of the situation.

Though power fell to the hands of the Soviet party like ripened fruit, there was yet before it the task of making sure its hold. It had to rid itself of its enemies if its tenure was to be secure. The Soviet forces, not inclined to gentleness by nature, did not refrain from the sternest, even brutal, measures, in putting down all opposition. To those who stood in their way they showed little pity or mercy. They had been used to receiving violence at the hands of those who oppressed them; now that the seat of power was with them, they were prepared to deal out violence. All enemies of the new order who remained in the land must be brought low and rendered harmless to it. It must be seen that the new government was neither overthrown nor undermined.

To make sure that their authority did not collapse, the

Soviet leaders had the further task of making food and industrial products available to the people. They proceeded without delay and without remorse to seize and take over whatever private wealth was left in the land. This was hardly to be attained without the exercise of physical compulsion; and violence again reigned.

In dealing with enemies or obstructionists of any kind, the Soviet power proceeded without knowledge of compassion. Its work was attended with outbursts of savagery. Individual or wholesale massacres became the order of the day. In making its place secure, the Soviet régime launched itself in a sea of blood. There was a "Red" terror that no man might forget. But however bitter the conflict, it was the Soviet authority that emerged victor.

Competent as was the Soviet party to take over power, it was no less competent at wielding power when once in its hands. And with power it was ready to exercise a ruthless dictatorship, giving no other party or group any chance of contesting its rule. Shortly after the revolution a so-called constituent assembly was created, which came nearer to representing the masses of the population of Russia than any body yet created; the Soviet party was greatly outnumbered, and should have yielded up its power. But it did no such thing. By sheer force it held on. It was a victory of the city worker, perhaps a bit more clever and a bit more adept in organization or in mass movements than the crude and stolid peasant from the country. The despotism thus inaugurated by the Soviet party has been maintained down to this day.

The power of the Soviet forces was solidified by certain happenings at the time, for which they were not responsible, but which served to put them in high feather. But for these occurrences it is just possible that the government might have been wrested from their hands. After the Soviet party had taken control of the old Russian

Empire, attempts were made by incensed "White Russians" to drive it out and to repossess the land. In these movements there was sometimes aid or instigation from the Allies who had fought the World War. Through it was brought about an old situation in the history of nations —when a nation is invaded by armies from outside, it turns instinctively to any defenders it may have from within, no matter what its feelings may have previously been towards them. There was repeated in Russia what had happened in France just after its revolution when soldiers in the uniforms of foreign sovereigns moved upon the land. What the Allies, together with the "White Russians," did, played directly into the hands of the Soviet party. This intervention, whether wrongly conceived or not, only served to give Bolshevist arms strength and prestige.

From one direction and another the White armies advanced upon the country, and at times succeeded in penetrating far within. But they were too much consumed with rage and with desire for vengeance; and upon helpless and innocent inhabitants of the countryside and the towns occupied by them fell maddened onslaughts. Not always with discrimination in the matter of possible aid and comfort to the Bolshevist forces, men and women were tortured and executed, and their possessions seized. The old order, it was believed, was largely to be restored. There was a "White terror" in Russia no less than a "Red terror." The actions of the "White" Russians proved fatal to them; there were evoked toward them resentment and antagonism. The population of the territory invaded was made to turn as to friends to those who had tried to protect them and their country, and to regard them as their real friends. These were none other than the Bolsheviki. Nor were the Bolsheviki slow to take advantage of the situation and to turn it to good account. It was this stroke of fortune that gave them a grip upon the country as a whole that otherwise they could scarcely have had.

A very severe loss resulted to Russia, however, in the expatriation of a great number of her best and worthiest citizens. All over Europe and in other parts of the world are still exiled men and women who love and cherish their native land despite its revolution and its present governing party. Many have experienced keen suffering through what has transpired; many have lost their all. A large part cannot return to Russia; or, if so, only with the loss of their self-respect. As with other countries in the world's history, persecution at home has driven into the arms of other lands some of the choicest of the population.

At the same time there are some former Russians out of the country that Russia, or any other nation, is better off without. These are persons who have a blind hatred towards those who differ with them—certainly as great a hatred as had the Bolsheviki. If they could once secure control of the government, they would have little beyond a spirit of vindictiveness, which very likely would vent itself upon quiet, inoffensive citizens as well as upon active enemies. In addition, not a few of them would be imbued mainly with a desire for the exploitation of the land for their own private benefit. Such emigrés are of the kind who learn nothing and forgive nothing.

CHAPTER VI

SOVIET ACCOMPLISHMENTS AND SOVIET OPERATIONS

IN THEORY the organization of the Soviet government which has been set up is far from being a bad one. Beginning with the lowest or smallest unit, which in industrial areas is made up of occupational groups, and in rural areas of territorial groups, delegates are elected to a higher and larger one, and so on, till the official government at Moscow is constituted. The system is thus a pyramided one, rising tier above tier. Recognition is given to one's standing alike as a citizen and as a producer. There is left much local self-government, or cultural autonomy. Questions of a strictly domestic nature are passed upon by the different republics or other units. (A republic is given the formal right to withdraw from the Union.)

The government finally emerging, as now definitely established, consists of a union congress or parliament, known as the supreme soviet, which is made up of two bodies of equal power, one a union council based upon and representing the entire land, and the other a council of nationalities, with delegates duly apportioned among the several political divisions, higher divisions having more, and lower less. By the parliament is elected a central executive committee, or presidium, consisting of a president, some half score vice-presidents, and a score of other officials, including heads of departments or commissariats, all an executive committee of wide powers, formulating broad principles of legislation, and carrying on the general administration of government. There is in addition a graduated judiciary, including a supreme court. Smaller political divisions have an analogous or corresponding set-up.

There are a number of commissars (Council of People's Commissars), appointed by the central executive committee, who are vested with immediate administrative powers. For the general union they act for defense, foreign affairs, foreign trade, railways, communications, water transportation, heavy industries. For the smaller units they act for light industries, food industries, timber industries, agriculture, state farms, internal affairs, internal trade, finance, public health, justice. The central government has broad powers—over international relations (including war, trade, etc.), admission of new areas, boundaries, citizenship, national economy, judiciary, banking, currency, natural resources, agriculture, education, health, labor, crime, etc.

The whole scheme is by authorization and direction of the constitution of the land. To students of political science the plan of government of the Union of Soviet Socialist Republics, novel though it is to our ears, has some quite desirable features; there are few who would condemn it altogether.

The leaders of Soviet Russia are not to be set down as a lot of malevolent or unprincipled or unscrupulous men. Not a few are highly educated, widely read, acquainted with the social sciences, and versed in the doings of the world and of men; not a few are men of talent and ability; not a few are of the devoted, high-minded type. In nearly all, however, there has been a narrowness of vision, a distorted, perverted outlook, a dogmatic, intolerant attitude, and a bitterness of spirit towards those in the rest of the world who dare to differ with them.

What has made the Soviet movement of such grave concern and of such potential danger, not only within its own borders, but to the whole world, even if not so pronounced today as formerly, has been this flaming intolerance towards all those who do not share its views and principles—or towards all those who do not see eye to eye politically with those who happen to be in the seats of Soviet power. To the Soviet people, especially in the early days, there was preached an everlasting, truceless war against the foes of communism; into their hearts was burned a class hatred, bitter, implacable, ready to stop at nothing. Upon the Soviet people was enjoined the utter destruction, the extermination of the "enemies of the revolution"; they were charged to be relentless and pitiless toward these enemies. It is this attitude that rendered the Soviet power a thing of ferocity within its land, and a thing possibly boding ill for the world in general. In respect to such a frame of mind, furthermore, one may ask if the Soviet order is not being built upon the point of bayonets; and if a state of war is not being entered upon, a war from which there is to be no surcease, the combatants perhaps merely changing positions.

In the setting up of the Soviet empire the influence of Germany has been marked. In not a few respects the Soviet leaders admired the neighboring country to the west, and decided to go that country one better. In more ways than one they have taken Germany as a model. They have taken over, greatly extended, in a sense perfected, and clamped down harder the state socialism there found. They have followed and adapted German social welfare measures, including general care of the physical well-being and health of the people. They have linked up production, in greater degree, with the needs of the state, including military needs. They have been prepared to utilize national manpower for state ends. They have attached high value to the museum in popular education. They have integrated technical education with general education. They have made the school a powerful tool for inculcating complete subservience to the will of the state. They have placed immense if not infinite faith in science, something so characteristic of the German nation. Above all, they have adopted forthright the iron discipline of that nation. Soviet Russia and present-day Germany are not separated by a wide gulf in their attitudes towards absolutism in government, or in what we sometimes call totalitarianism.

Let us set down without reservation the things that have been done to the credit of Soviet Russia. It has secured some sort of order in a land thrown into confusion and chaos. It has moved the capital back to Moscow— a rare stroke of policy. It has made the country a union of self-governing states within their own confines, instead of a highly concentrated government at a distant capital (except as to general national policies). It has lent encouragement to backward peoples, and has developed their local resources. It has provided a government for them adapted somewhat to their present cultural levels and to their political maturity. It has greatly diminished if not abolished racial prejudices and animosities. It has put an end to Jewish persecutions and pogroms. It has sought to preserve and promote a national culture.

It has prevented the exploitation by private interests of the natural resources of the land, and has kept them for the benefit of the people. It has taken up the systematic development of these vast natural resources, seeking their discovery and their use to the greatest possible degree. It has undertaken the industrial rehabilitation of the country. It has caused its industrialization to proceed at a rapid pace. It has introduced new and more efficient methods of winning the harvest from the soil. It has insisted upon the highest possible productivity in the land, in agriculture and industry alike. It has recognized the importance of research, with some notable results in agriculture and elsewhere. It has had great industrial structures rear their heads over the land, and has some genuine engineering triumphs to its credit. It has made valuable extensions of hydraulic power. It has achieved considerable progress in irrigation, with the lessening of the effects of droughts. It has promoted reforestation and swamp drainage. It has demonstrated the advantages of coöperative attitudes in agricultural production. It has called attention to the possible value of state planning in respect to the production of goods. It has called attention to the possibilities of the reduction of costs of goods through the elimination of competitive advertising and middlemen. It has set forth a social motive in the production of articles to be consumed by the people. It has made progress in the stabilization of the currency, and has thwarted the prostration of its money and banking system, under remarkable and hitherto untried conditions.

It has highly recognized the importance of education, including vocational education, and has sought to bring a degree of education and of culture to all the people. It has established additional universities and technical schools. It has sought to make graduates of its institutions of higher education realize the obligations resting upon them to serve the public. It has reformed the calendar, has adopted western systems of measurement, and promises in due time to take over the Latin alphabet. It has sought to provide recreation and entertainment of some kind for the masses. It has sought to eliminate extravagance and display in the state. It has sought to

eliminate graft and corruption in government. It has
sought physical health and efficiency for the people, and
the cultivation of the hardy virtues.

It has sought to introduce humanitarian conceptions
in policies of the state. It has instituted a noteworthy
program of prison reform. It has created rest and recuper-
ation centers for sick and disabled workers. It has sought
to give the economically weak a chance, and to forestall
their economic exploitation. It has sought to give labor
a dignity not merely in words, but also to show values in
it not to be measured by the goods produced—goods perhaps produced with mutual help—and it has rendered
public honor for services rendered. It has given all a
chance to share in the wealth of the land in return for
some labor. It has given women a new and more notable
part in the life of the state.

There has, furthermore, arisen throughout the land a
certain fellow feeling, a comradeship, if not in full measure, at least in considerable degree, and even if approaching a pale uniformity, or dipping towards a dead levelism
—something to take the place of the old hateful system
of a handful of nobility living on the fat of the land and
the vast masses writhing under foot.

Possibly the greatest thing that has come to the people of Soviet Russia since the old Czaristic days has been
the changed outlook upon life, perhaps largely of psycho-
logical bearings, but none the less of much significance.
Instead of the paralyzed, deadened masses of former
years, there is to a wide extent a people interested in the
life about them, alert, stirring, animated with a genuine
enthusiasm for some of the undertakings in which they
are engaged, with a greater respect for themselves, and
with a wistful hope for better things. Perhaps there has
been a groping for the light.

A very important contribution which Soviet Russia

has made to the thinking of the world in general, and which may have no less application there, lies in its theories of progress. The Soviet state has unlimited faith in the possibilities of human betterment. If success, it declares, is to attend its efforts, and if it is to move toward a truly communistic state, use will have to be made of all of the science, art, technique, and experience of the human race. In particular it places vast trust in the power and efficiency of the industrial machine—including constant technological improvement and wide progress in electrification over the country—in the production of wealth and in making possible a "good life" for all the people. In contemplation of such results it is taking cognizance of the amount of leisure time which is to be at the disposal of the people, and seeks to make provision for putting to account this leisure.

Soviet Russia has surprised the world by showing, not that its policy was a largely negative one, but that it had a positive and constructive program. For not a few matters it has demonstrated quite a statesmanlike attitude. While some of the industrial operations have often shown crudity or haste, others have shown resourcefulness, or even ingenuity; in a great number there has been displayed ample zeal.

All the more credit may be given in view of the situation which has had to be faced. There was the immense, almost incalculable difficulty of adapting socialism to a large agricultural country like Russia, with its great number of peasant proprietors naturally averse to the extension of the policy to their holdings. There was widespread poverty in the land, with little capital to start any sort of operations. There was little enlightened counsel or guidance to be had, and limited skilled direction, especially for the organization of industry. For great undertakings there had to be employed a labor force of little technical experience and with little discipline. (Soviet Russia did not, however, have to start out industrially altogether from scratch; it had left over from Czaristic days a small number of technicians, some factories, and some acquaintance with such matters as agricultural coöperation, factory regulation, and social insurance.) But whatever Soviet Russia accomplished, it had to accomplish alone; it could expect little of encouragement, of coöperation, or of good-will from other lands.

Great care must be exercised in appraising, from the economic standpoint, the concrete, material results, but it may be said in general that, compared with former times in Russia, there has been a certain improvement in industrial and living conditions—a matter to receive later attention. If actual wages paid into the hands of the workers may not have changed so much for the better, it is to be remembered that a great deal is being done for them by the state which otherwise, if secured at all, would have to be at the expense of the individual.

What success, however, has been attained in Soviet Russia, or whatever of credit is to be set down for it, is to be tempered by several circumstances. In the first place, the Soviet government has had a relatively clean slate to work upon—one that only an autocratic government can have at its disposal. There has been no serious opposition which has had to be taken in hand. There has been little to stay the execution of whatever policies the government has adopted. To make matters the easier for it, the people over which it has ruled have been singularly unenlightened and unresisting. Never was there such an amorphous mass ready for the moulding.

It is by no means certain that whatever improvements or reforms or beneficial developments have taken place in Soviet Russia could not have been undertaken just as well under a different form of government, and quite possibly with more solid results. Russia has been part of a world engaged in general reorganization and development. Whatever occurs in Russia under Soviet direction, with its socialist bearings, is made to appear of spectacular nature and is heralded with loud acclaim. In Turkey, by way of example, far-reaching reforms have been instituted without any such fanfare. Certainly, also, in the quondam neighboring states that were carved out of old Russia— Poland, Lithuania, Latvia, and Estonia, together with still quasi-independent Finland—great developments have taken place. Here was abundant evidence of the progress of independent, enlightened nations. On all sides one found industrial and agricultural development, the promotion of markets, the building of schools, social welfare legislation, coöperative societies (especially consumers' societies and agricultural societies), government-promoted housing for the people on a wide scale, and so on. Some of these lands had high achievements to their credit. Their record of progress was often truly an inspiring one. But what they did was not with the flourish or with the high-sounding language of Soviet Russia.

It is to be remembered, moreover, that some activities of a socialist nature in Russia are different from those in other countries of Europe in degree rather than in kind. In nearly all the countries of the Continent there is state socialism to a greater or less extent. This includes government ownership of means of transportation and communication (railroads and waterways, as well as telegraph and telephone facilities), besides a large part of the forest reserves and other natural resources. These things are taken as a matter of course, and there is virtually no organized opposition to them.

One of the best tests as to the possible success of the operations of the Soviet government is to be found in the attitude of the people of other lands, especially adjacent lands, towards it, and in the extent of their desire to secure a like government. In the states that have been created out of old Russia, and that became independent of it at the time the revolution was effected there, there could be discovered no great leaning toward its political and economic system, or any pronounced yearning to repeat Russia's experiment in their own territory. The condition of the industrial and farming population in these countries was on the whole probably a bit above that in Soviet Russia; and probably no large portion would have favored following in the footsteps. As a matter of fact, from the time of the revolution on to today the great hope and prayer of the people in general in the neighboring lands may be said to have been that Soviet Russia might not, by the exercise of its military might or otherwise, be permitted to overcome them and impose upon them its political and economic system. Over Europe generally the cause of communism can hardly be declared to have gained ground in consequence of the experiments in Russia.

Of the final outcome of the socialist undertaking now in progress in Russia, no one can speak with certainty. The issue of the matter lies in the lap of the gods.

In Soviet Russia at hand was the vast experiment of which the world had dreamed and for which it was waiting —the possibility of a coöperative society, a state order, in which the profit motive and the profit system were not to be the controlling factors in the affairs of men. There were envisaged some of the noblest ideals that have ever come to the mind of man—a society organized in such fashion that those foremost considerations of human existence, wealth, leisure, and the means of happiness— what philosophers have long called the "good life"— should not be left or confined to a small, limited section or class of the population, but should be shared by all, including the masses, and including more particularly those who perform useful labor and who supply the human element for the creation of wealth. How near Soviet Russia came to this high goal, or how far distant it remained from it, will long be debated among men.

In the inauguration of the new program, some matters might move along lines relatively simple, some along lines more difficult and complex. If in its economic aspects the experiment was to proceed according to the sound Marxian gospel, there must always be consideration of the fact that the country was largely an agricultural one, and one not adaptable off-hand to a socialist program.

A new régime could not have started off less auspiciously, matters could not have been worse for a new political organization arriving upon the scene or taking over the reins of government, than was the case when the Soviets came to power. The country was truly exhausted after its part in the World War, though it had deserted its allies, and had secured a patched-up peace with its former foes. At the conclusion of this war it had to face a counter revolution undertaken by the enemies of the new order. When both these war clouds had been dissipated, not only had a vast amount of the wealth of the country been destroyed but great numbers also of its agricultural and industrial workers had been killed, maimed, or otherwise lost. The transportation system had almost completely broken down. There was a shortage of food, and also of fuel and materials. The productiveness of the country, never at a high ebb, was brought very low. Agriculture, which had never been of an efficient order, was hardly in position to meet the present fresh demands upon it. Many of the ablest business engineers had fled the land.

Food supplies at the beginning did not suffice for the population, decimated though it was. In many areas food was not to be had, or was to be had with great difficulty.

Factories were run down, and the goods that could be turned out by them were far below what was required. Industry was, in fact, almost at a standstill. Crop failures in the early days made the situation worse and augmented the country's woes. At times the country was all but stripped of food. Rationing of food in the cities had to be introduced. Starvation stalked the land and many fell its victims. Suffering was widespread and acute.

At the outset all the available food was requisitioned by the Soviet authorities; it was to feed the army, and as far as possible the rest of the population that was in dire need. Grain, live stock, and other foodstuffs were taken from the peasants, possibly with promise of payment, but really confiscated, to be distributed among those in want. This treatment was resented by the peasants, who proceeded to cut down production to avoid handing over the fruit of their toil without recompense. Part of their land they refused to cultivate; part of their products they hid or destroyed. There were even peasant uprisings. A particular source of grievance with the peasants was the taking of much of their food for the benefit of the city dwellers, who, the peasants always believed, were being benefited at their expense, and constituted a favored class in the Soviet economy. For a long time the peasants, if not hostile to the Soviet régime, were critical of it.

After a few years the government decided to abolish the levies upon the produce of the peasants; instead a tax was imposed. To avoid giving further offense to this class, as well as for other reasons, trade, which had at first been forbidden in the land, was permitted to an extent; surplus products might be sold on private markets.

The government also turned to the encouraging and promoting of agricultural coöperative bodies, consumers' coöperative bodies, and marketing coöperative bodies, especially with respect to the necessaries of life.

In the early days of the Soviet undertaking there had to be a certain departure from strict socialist doctrines. The exigencies of the situation did not permit complete adherence to them. There had to be a greater or less loosening of the rigid precepts for the time being, and some sort of adjustment to the conditions actually being faced.

Because of the lack of sufficient engineering talent, the Soviet government for a time farmed out or allowed as concessions to private capitalists the inauguration or operation of certain enterprises, especially those for the development of some natural resource or for the production of necessary articles or for the promotion of some particular form of trade. The government kept a firm hand on all the proceedings; as a rule when it had paid back the costs of the investment, the physical equipment was left on Russian soil, and the country was that much better off. After a little time, all natural resources were to be exploited exclusively by the state. They were for a greater or less length of time to be in the hands of what were called state trusts. Such was the disposition also of the larger industries.

In consequence, furthermore, of the crude, well-nigh chaotic conditions existing in these first years, when the new government was getting on its feet and something had to be done to meet pressing, imperative needs, and for the very preservation of the life of the new state, a measure of private activities had to be allowed. Certain concessions had, as we have seen, to be made to peasants, and also to certain kinds of traders, for the securing of necessary consumer goods. Some private land might be rented, and some labor hired. Products might be sold to private dealers, to be disposed of as they could. Idle factories of inconsiderable capacity might be leased to private operators. Other business undertakings of limited character might for the time being revert to private hands. It was the fairly well-to-do peasant, the middleman, the retail dealer, and the small industrialist who took advantage of the procedure. But these did not fare so well on the whole. Whatever prosperity they might enjoy—which after all was not great—they did not win general favor or popularity. They had rather denunciation and upbraiding for their non-communistic behavior. They were under suspicion; their doings did not escape the eyes of the state. Civil rights in greater or less measure could be taken away. Particular evidence of affluence could be countered by extra taxation.

The "new economic policy," as it was called, though relatively brief (lasting less than a decade) and intended only as a transitory measure, seemed like a return to capitalism, and by many was so hailed. It was, however, to be looked upon as a respite in the Soviet over-hasty procedure; more than that, it could afford opportunity for educating in socialist principles the people of the land, especially the peasants, who had found the movements a little too rapid, and who had never become completely reconciled to the new order.

Without doubt the indulgence on the part of the Soviet state that had been granted to certain groups in the population gave it a breathing spell, and tided it over these critical days. During this period it was enabled to make a study of general conditions and needs in the country, to consolidate its internal positions, and to effect some measure of economic reconstruction. In due time, and after only a few years, all such private enterprises were barred. The state trusts that had been called into being to manage state industries were taking the field—to be followed by planning systems by which within a given period production was to be placed under specified bounds.

Thus to an extent or in some respects Soviet Russia in

its industrial launching followed the technique of capitalism. But while such procedure may have been contrary to the teachings of orthodox socialism, it need not
have been taken as subversive thereof, or as the entering
wedge for the return of capitalism. Modifications of or
compromises with socialistic principles were only temporary expedients; they did not prove fatal.

The Soviet land was now committed to the socialist system and that system was now to set in. Fairly rapidly the
socialist tide closed in upon the land. The three great
desiderata of socialism—no interest, no rent, no profit—
have been or are in the way of being achieved in the Soviet
socialist state.

At the outset attempt was made to "nationalize" all
the private property in the land that was to come under
the state's control, a procedure that continued apace till
the goal was entirely or substantially achieved.

Private property is now allowed in one's dwelling, fur-
nishings, earnings, savings, and articles of personal consumption; and these may be inherited. Collective farm
groups may own their farms and appurtenances. No
private property may be used for the production of further
wealth. Accumulation of wealth that is not directly earned
is under definite ban.

Wealth that smacked of private capital, whether the
owner lived in Russia or had moved away, could be ex-
propriated readily enough by the state. For the small
capitalist who resided within, there was always at hand a
convenient means of liquidation—the inescapable vehicle
of taxation—if there were not evoked more direct or more
drastic methods.

Means of production, transportation, and distribution of
wealth could to a considerable extent pass into the hands
of the state fairly smoothly, without too great violence or
upheaval and with less of disturbance in the transition

period to the general national economy. Their taking over
could be regarded as the most natural or most logical
movement in the whole process. State ownership, as we
have seen, had already applied in Russia as well as in
other continental countries to common carriers and public
utilities. Manufacturing establishments controlled by
capitalists, foreign or domestic, could be physically appropriated without too much distress to the Soviet conscience.
Their "nationalization" presented industrial rather than
political difficulties. "Nationalization" of the farms was
a quite different and a far more serious matter, as we are
later to see.

Political subdivisions or local communities are now
encouraged to attend to their own economic wants which
are of small-scale and relatively simple nature, thus reduc-
ing possible cityward migration and highway and railway
congestion; larger industrial enterprises are left to the
central state authorities.

Trade was, on the whole, a little more gradual in passing
from private hands, or in suffering "liquidation." Foreign
trade was of course a government monopoly from the beginning. Private trade in a small way was, as has been
indicated, permitted for a time. One was allowed to sell or
market one's own products; there was limited capitalism
on the farm or in a modest industry. But all this was only
a temporary makeshift. Practically always whatever small
and restricted business and commercial undertakings were
privately owned, had to face state competition and the
possibility of state expropriation, apart from any difficulties a local private dealer might have in getting stock or
supplies from the proper state agency, or in getting credit,
and apart from more or less heavy taxation. For none
did the outlook appear bright; and it was not long before
their fate overtook them. Stores are now mostly state-
owned, in general in the hands of a state trust, commis-
sariat, or similar state organization. (Trusts, somewhat

like corporations in capitalist countries, but with the shares of stock mainly in the hands of the state, have been largely organizations for the production of goods. For the purpose of supplying raw materials, conducting trade and marketing, and securing credit, there have been created what have been known as syndicates, perhaps involving unification or coördination between certain trusts. Syndicates may pass into combines, of even larger scope, and to an extent on the order of holding companies in America.) Some stores are in the hands of industrial establishments. Shops of several different kinds have been possible, some containing goods of better quality or of wider variety than others, and open to different classes of purchasers. Prevailing is the "chain store."

Where direct state action might be wanting, there has been something close to it in the coöperative associations —not the independent movements found in other lands, but in Soviet Russia an immediate link in the socialist machine. Coöperative bodies here are in fact in a sort of twilight zone between capitalism and socialism—on the one hand, with shares acquired by individual citizens and with due participation in accruing gains, and, on the other hand, with greater or less direction and control by the state and with the economic exploitation of no individual. Such bodies receive much encouragement and assistance from the state; advantages of membership are constantly pointed out. They may expect materials of better quality to handle, lower taxes, lower transportation charges, less difficulty in securing credits. They have some features not unlike those of trade unions. Such associations may be of consumers, producers (particularly in respect to farm products and handicraft articles), and market dealers. Operations of some associations, especially of consumers, have been transferred more directly to the state.

For a long time in different parts of Russia there has

been home or village manufacture of simple articles of
one kind and another—woodwork, leather work, metal
work, linen work, embroidery, basketmaking, spinning and
weaving of wool, rug making, painting of small objects, etc.
These have had usually a considerable sale, largely local,
and for the most part without a very definite business organization. Such production has continued, though at a
diminishing rate, under the Soviet authority. Peddling of
articles of this nature or of articles not produced in a
regular factory has received a measure of toleration in the
Soviet land, though now rather giving way to the use of
permanent stands. In some areas a place, though a decreasing one, may be made for the open street sale, or for
markets, fairs, or bazaars, long a part of the old Russia.
Barter has by no means disappeared from trade in the
Soviet country.

Home craftsmen may thus in some measure ply their
trade; and small-scale manufacturing may be possible if
tacked into the state's general industrial activities. Those
persons who make articles of the description indicated are
free to sell them for whatever price they will bring, provided no profit accrues from the transaction; but even
here such activities may readily be swept into a coöperative body. Private trading through middlemen is of course
always barred. Private speculation in different commodi-
ties, or buying low and selling higher, it is also to be said,
persists to some degree; it has not altogether been done
away with. Transactions of this nature, however, are not
of great moment.

Repair work, the production of some homely commodity
made to order, or the performance of certain personal services (as with musicians, teachers, electricians, tailors,
shoemakers, etc.) is also permitted to the individual; an
extra penny may now and then in this manner be picked
up after the quota of one's state assignments has been

met—provided always that no "profit" is involved in the matter. In a profession like that of the physician private practice is theoretically possible, but only in competition with an all but complete system of state medicine. Private physicians, moreover, could hardly provide their necessary medical equipment. Professional persons in general can expect little private practice—only in the few odd hours when they are not in the service of the state. Private practitioners may always expect a special tax. They are also without the benefits attaching to trade unions or coöperative bodies. All such private activities are, in keeping with general Soviet trends, passing into state or coöperative activities.

Very early it was found that money and banks were things that could not well be dispensed with. Employment of money is, however, more restricted than is the case in capitalist countries. There is a general banking system, with many of the features and functions of banking systems in capitalist lands; but here it is under the immediate control and direction of the state, designed to promote its interests, and used mainly for its ends. Savings banks, with interest on deposits, are available for the citizens. In foreign trade and in general financial relations with other lands Soviet Russia has as a rule sought to live up to its obligations—despite the fact that the debts incurred under the reign of the Czar were repudiated.

Even in Soviet land interest is possible for money that is lent, but chiefly for the gain of the state and not for that of the individual. Rates of interest appear to be fair and reasonable. Loans may be made by the government, or by its banks, to state trusts, coöperative associations, trade unions, clubs, etc. Money may be lent to the government through the buying of bonds. (Lotteries are authorized by the state.) But let it not be thought that a Soviet citizen may thus acquire riches. Income in this country may not exceed certain limits; in addition, taxes are always at hand when one appears in possession of too much money. Income taxes are steeply progressive.

If the issue of socialism in Soviet Russia had been confined to the large cities, and there had been no outside complications, it might be said that it was unquestionably a going concern, had possibly proved a considerable success, certainly not an out-and-out failure. But when reference is made to the whole land, rural as well as urban, the story becomes somewhat different. At any rate it may be affirmed that socialist Russia has the negative virtue of not having collapsed; possibly considerably stronger and positive language may be used as to what has taken place so far. Whether the roots go down deep enough into the soil of human nature and world conditions to insure a favorable issue for the future, or how far general procedures and policies are built upon permanent foundations, are questions to which an answer is not to be had at the present moment. Whether, furthermore, the people who live under the existing system are happier and better off economically than they would be under some other, is likewise a question to which a reply is not now forthcoming.

CHAPTER VII

IMPACT OF THE SOCIALIST STATE UPON THE FARM

THE whole issue of Soviet socialism might have had a more favorable outcome, with greater assurance of success and stability, had not the rural situation in Russia had to be reckoned with. That country is essentially an agricultural land, with the bulk of its population, at least until more recent years, living on farms and away from the cities. From practically the beginning the Soviet authorities have been engaged in the "socialization" of this population, an undertaking bristling with difficulties and dangers of a kind unknown in the cities. The situation was made all the worse by what was told the country peasant at the commencement of the revolution. He was told that the great landed estates were to be broken up and placed in the hands of peasant proprietors, a process in which he had himself already been more or less engaged. It was this announcement and this promise that won over the peasant masses and caused them to cast in their allegiance with the Soviet party, or at least not to take a stand in opposition.

Later the peasant was told a different story. He was told that the products of his farm, which he felt were largely due to his bodily labor, were not to be his after all, for him to do with as he wished; but that they might be appropriated by the state. He also learned that the land which he thought was his might be taken over and joined in a great state farm, upon which, merely as an employee, he might be compelled to do whatever tasks were allotted him.

The great question in rural areas thus became of two-fold nature: whether the peasants might retain their own farmsteads if they wished; and whether those who wanted to save up something and have something which they might call their own, to be sold for such price as they saw fit, might do so. Could the peasants in general come to favor state or collective farms over their own private holdings? Would they consent to have no direct possession or ownership over what they might produce through their own efforts—something that they and their fathers had been used to? Here was being prepared the great battle-ground on which the issue of socialism in Russia was to be fought. Was it a struggle'at bottom against human nature, or against man's instinctive desire for the personal holding of land?

If state or collective farms should be generally established, and if they should attain a considerable measure of success, and if the farming population as a whole approves of the system, or at least acquiesces in it without serious objection, then the Soviet state will have a great achievement to its credit. But if this is brought about fundamentally through the use of force, the policy cannot be written down as a success; possibly quite the reverse.

The Soviet party was resolved that all peasant proprietors of whatever kind must go; it could not endure a "capitalistic" class even among the humble farmers of the country. When, however, it began the process of "liquidation," or of pressing all on the land into state or collective farms, it encountered violent opposition. There was little inclination on the part of the peasant farmer to surrender the property which he regarded as his own. Main resistance came from the "kulaks," a term not to be confined to "rich" peasants but to be applied to many who had been thrifty and relatively more skilled, and had become relatively well-to-do, including some who had lent money, rented agricultural implements, or had engaged in other local enterprises, and possibly some who in earlier days had been charged with being grasping and with oppressing and exploiting poorer neighbors. A considerable number of the peasants, even if not to be identified with the kulaks, were disposed to sympathize with them, not being greatly impressed by the class distinctions so vigorously insisted upon by the Soviet régime, and in many cases being bound to the kulaks by ties of friendship or even of blood.

These peasant farmers were suspected, and often rightly enough, of storing or hiding the products of their farms or other possessions. Agents of the government who sought to take these things were fought off, and at times came off second best. Sometimes the farmers disposed of what they had as best they could; if nothing better was at hand, destruction was possible, of grain and livestock alike. Sabotage was a weapon new to their hands, but one effectively employed. A portion decided that there was no hope for them on the farm, and left for the cities. All this followed attempts more or less unavailing on the part of the Soviet authorities to make the peasants see on their own account the value of collective farming, with promises of favors to be extended for compliance.

Pressure of all kinds was exercised upon the obstinate, recalcitrant farmers, and finally force was employed to make them yield. In a supreme effort to bring about capitulation, there was effected a mass removal of uncounted numbers from their homes. In the process some were slain, others fell by the way as they were shifted over the country, and others were deported or exiled to far distant regions where they were left to perish of cold or starvation or to meet other wretched ends—a tale without parallel in modern history, and one that will awaken the horror of ages to come. The Soviet state has never disavowed its willingness to sacrifice great numbers of its population to attain its goal, and has expressed no qualms with respect thereto.

Thus the farms of the peasant proprietors, the length and breadth of the land, were taken from them. They were absorbed or incorporated into larger farm institutions, all the creatures of the state.

These farms are in an ascending order according to the degree or extent of state control. There are three forms which involve a variety of collective ownership in the hands of a number pooling their land and working in common, but with general state oversight, direction, and planning. The lowest form is a sort of limited coöperative association, with the members individually living in their homes and coming together for joint agricultural purposes. The second form is that of a group living in individual homes but with the basic means of production held in common, and paid according to the labor performed by each. The third is a body where all live and work together, all property being held in common except certain personal property, and where all share the proceeds of their joint endeavors—approaching more distinctly a real communal arrangement. There is also a fourth form, the highest of all, which constitutes the culmination of the system, a state farm directly in the hands of the government, organized and operating much as a state factory. This last, however, has appeared less advantageous and promising than the others, though it may be used to a considerable extent as an agricultural laboratory or experiment station. The second form, or that where land, buildings, animals, implements, etc., are jointly owned, but not the homes of the different workers, is regarded as the most efficient and on the whole the most desirable one. This form, which is a degree less than fully communal, or under full state control, would indicate a certain recognition of the value of one's having his own home in which to live. An individually owned farm, however, would not fare so well: it would have to face heavy taxation, difficulties in securing the use of tractors, and other obstacles. Some small farms still exist, but in a steadily decreasing number.

In these farms as a general thing a designated part of the total produce is assigned to the government, together with the tax that has been levied, and together with a charge for the use of tractors and other machinery that have been provided (there being machine and tractor stations, each serving farms in a given area) and for advice given or other special service. What is left is distributed among the various workers according to the work done by each. As with factories, there may be penalties for laggards, and bonuses or premiums for the more energetic. On the farms agricultural implements have not always been of the best, and, particularly in the earlier years, have been far from adequate. Breakdowns and fuel shortages have not been unknown. Compulsory insurance applies to farm buildings, crops, and live stock, as well as to industrial establishments, homes, etc.

Of late years local resentment and animosity on the part of the farmers have been moderated somewhat as a result of the increased prosperity of the collective farms, with less objection to the pooling process. This situation is due in particular to the employment of modern machinery, with a more abundant food supply available and improved agricultural methods, with less drudgery on the part of the individual, and with less likelihood of a food shortage for the country as a whole. It has been found that with tractors earlier and deeper plowing is possible, and with better and hardier grain. In addition, peasants have been taught the value of proper seeds, incubation methods, means of combating insect pests, scientific stock raising. Grain growing has been extended to distant northern and semi-arid steppe regions.

With some portion of the farming population there has been a growing opinion that the returns from small iso-lated holdings in the hands of ignorant, starveling peasants could hardly be expected to equal those of a large-scale farming enterprise; the latter at the same time serving as a model and affording greater opportunities for education in proper farm operations. A highly mollifying influence upon the attitude of the farmers within more recent years has been the permitting of the cultivation about the home of a little plot of ground for a garden or orchard for the production of food for the consumption of the family, together with a cow or two, a few pigs, and some poultry, but no draft animals—a concession to private ownership of pretty considerable significance. To some industrial workers space near their dwellings may be allowed for similar purposes.

The struggle, however, between the peasant farmer and the state is by no means over. From time to time it is charged that the farmers are not doing their part on the collective farms, perhaps idling or trifling upon them, or that they are taking more than their share of the products. They are not infrequently said to be more concerned with their own private operations than with the business of the state—to be giving too much time to their own garden or pigs. Some are even declared to be renting out part of their limited domain—a restoration of landlordism on a small scale. Others are asserted to be engaged in a sort of buying or selling of surplus land, or land not supposed to be bought or sold—a species of speculation of distinctly capitalistic color. Still others are alleged to be hiring work-ers upon their tracts of land—a practice no less socialistically reprehensible. Some are accused of taking advantage of what is offered by membership in collective farms to escape taxation in some way. Because of too great a devotion to their own holdings on the part of the farmers, there may be an actual shortage of labor on the general farms. On their side, the farmers claim that the share of the products demanded by the state is often quite too large. Nor have they given up the belief, cherished by them from the beginning, that they have been discriminated against in favor of the city dwellers. Some of the peasant farmers leave the country of their own accord, usually going to the city to swell its population. Some are forcibly taken away in case a sparse farm population in other regions requires additional labor.

Although the collective farm under the general direction of the state is doubtless stronger in Soviet Russia than before, many undoubtedly still harbor the old resentments. Perhaps it is too much to ask of human nature that it abandon an age-old persuasion that a freehold, a little space around one's home, should be one's own, immune from outside interference of any sort, even that of the state. Perhaps there is also the fear that an agricultural serfdom is being established in the land. Finally, it is easy to recall the fate of those who in the beginning protested against such things and had to suffer outrageously in consequence. Should the peasants in general resign themselves to the policy of farm collectivization, they will probably demand a larger voice in government and in the disposal of their products.

CHAPTER VIII

PRODUCTION IN THE SOVIET STATE

THE industrial organization and operation of state farms and factories have much in common. Both farm and factory are something more than producing units; they combine cultural and social features— the larger maintaining health centers, educational centers, etc. The large coöperative or state farm may have upon it or near it a nucleus or center for agricultural operations and thus take on the appearance of a small village. Spreading out from it will be found clubs, schools, nurseries, theaters, hospitals, libraries, stores, laundries, bakeries, power plants, sheds, stables, etc. Some peasants go from the village to the farm to work as of old. In the Soviet language farms may be called grain factories or agronomic culture centers.

In the factories organization is carried to higher levels still. Here the trade unions—which are found in all industries and given every encouragement and which are practically an arm of the state—are concerned not only with wages and hours and accident prevention and with social insurance in general, but also with such things as recreation, education, and housing for their members. They intertwine with the equally ubiquitous clubs which have a considerable part in taking care of the leisure time of the workers—for with the relatively short working day much leisure time is to be available. The trade union is rather concerned with industrial conditions; the club, with recreational and cultural activities. As with coöperative associations, there are special inducements for joining the trade unions—lower taxes, lower rents, cheaper tickets at entertainments, etc.—apart from social insurance benefits.

In the Soviet land great stress has been placed upon state planning of production. For five or ten year periods definite production goals have been set for both manufactured articles and farm produce, and intensive, even feverish, efforts have been made to speed up production in order to reach the desired goals within the allotted time. One particular purpose has been to attain national self-sufficiency and to catch up economically with the more industrial capitalistic lands, or at least to reduce in some degree the inequalities between Soviet Russia and those other countries. Under such a planning program, the amount of goods to be produced was to be definitely ascertained and industry regulated accordingly; there was to be no slump, no depression, no crisis, no waste. A balance is struck between consumption and production. The state would also decide what community consumption to encourage and what to discourage. A not unimportant incidental expectation is that, with increased production of goods, higher standards of living will be possible for the people.

The outcome of this procedure in Soviet Russia has been varied. On the whole much has been accomplished in a relatively brief period, even though the products may have been of rather inferior quality; there have been notable strides toward state industrialism. By this method industry has undoubtedly been considerably benefited. All in all, there has been an increase in goods, including in particular certain goods of which the country was much in need, such as agricultural implements and automobiles. Standards of living have been raised somewhat. In some instances there has been a considerable measure of success, even though not all that was hoped for; in other instances the results have amounted to little. But though speed has been gained, it has not been without the accompaniment of privation and distress. The whole project was declared to have been paid for by decreased consumption power in general and by peasants' taxes. Because of the desire for speed, not a little of the machinery and materials in the factories was seriously injured. Just how far, in general, the nation has been set forward; how far scarcity in particular fields has been relieved or prevented; how far the hardships and sacrifices imposed have been justified; and how far the whole matter has been affected by the conditions peculiar to the country—cannot readily be determined.

The question of state planning is a very large one, with some indubitably good points, and with some not so much to be commended. Our approval or disapproval will depend in no small degree upon what we regard as sound economic principles or elementary economic laws, upon what we feel should or should not be left in government hands, and upon our possible belief that in such procedure there are too many factors lying in the future which cannot be foreseen. A socialist state is always in the best relative position to undertake state planning, for, like a gigantic corporation, it has under its control all the means of production. Certainly Soviet Russia's daring initiation of a new policy in shaping its economic order has compelled attention. Unfortunately for it, even with these bold attempts, hampered no doubt by many factors, production in Russia has lagged in comparison with that in other lands.

The people of the Soviet country have insisted upon high production; they have been demanding more and more of the satisfactions of life. Workers are constantly exhorted to increase production—even by wayside posters. The people have proved willing even if slow learners. Nor have they been reluctant to call in experts from out-

side, particularly from the United States. As Germany
has been taken somewhat as a model in state socialism, so
America has been taken as a model in industrial production, notably in work with railways, steel, and automobiles.
And the wealth of the Soviet country has increased in
greater or less measure.

As in capitalist countries, a troublesome situation is
liable to arise from technological progress, from the constant effort to substitute the machine for human labor—
to get rid of muscular toil as far as possible. If this is
carried too far, and if redistribution and readjustment of
human labor are not properly provided for in the process,
will there be enough jobs for all? If, furthermore, to
afford more jobs, hours of labor are reduced too far, will
there be assurance of sufficient production? And, finally,
how far can an efficient productive force be guaranteed
if living levels are not substantially raised? Such questions the Soviet people must ponder.

Legal regulations and rules governing labor in Russia
have been made quite favorable to the workers. Measures
for their protection, for their safety and comfort, are of
a high order. The working week has returned to one of
seven days—after attempts to make it basically one of
six days, or even of five days—with one day free from
labor for each individual. Work has at times been stag-
gered, a process that has permitted it to proceed regardless of the calendar, and regardless of the free time of
one's fellow workers, but also with continuous, unbroken
production. Normal hours of labor per day have been
fixed at eight, though formerly at seven. A forty-eight
hour week has not been uncommon. With reduced working hours as the accepted program in the Soviet state,
production may be more or less retarded. It is to be
expected, however, that this schedule will from time to
time, in emergencies or as the circumstances require, give

way to longer working periods. A two-week vacation during the year with pay has been the rule. Women may not engage in certain very heavy or arduous tasks, though these may be much more strenuous than is the case with women in other lands. There are fairly high standards for child labor. Children may not engage in remunerative toil until they are sixteen years of age or over, though there may be exception for those from fourteen to sixteen in particular circumstances, in which event their hours are to be shorter. Those from sixteen to eighteen are to be regarded in the light of apprentices, with their hours also somewhat reduced. None under eighteen, and no women at all, may engage in dangerous trades. Night work is similarly restricted. Wages and hours may vary according to the hazards involved in one's work. Social insurance provisions are liberal, the employer (the state or an agency of the state) paying premiums and costs.

Full provision is made for collective bargaining. The agreement here is, as might be expected, an elaborate affair, covering many matters, and with rigid regulations for the protection of the rights of the workers, which include wages, hours, general working conditions, overtime labor, rest periods, safety, inspection, etc. The agreement is between the labor union on one side, which is not other than an arm or branch of the state, and, on the other side, some agency or department of the government concerned with production—an odd, anomalous arrangement, but one not outside the logic of Soviet reasoning. The situation may become all the more peculiar because of the presence of a third party, the representative of the Communist party, who, still more strangely, may be serving in one of the two other capacities. As the government directs the whole proceedings, it may happen that the labor unions, despite their vaunted powers, are at times, especially when production is to be accelerated, hardly more than puppets; in such case there may not be too much scruple about disregarding some of the provisions of the labor agreement, the unions having no recourse other than to do the bidding of those in power. Labor discipline may be very severe; it may be tightened according to the exigencies of a particular situation. To foremen has been given increased authority. For spoiled goods the worker may receive no pay. For waste, loafing, shirking, inefficiency, misbehavior, absence, or tardiness a penalty may be imposed—public reprimand, demotion, dismissal, withholding of wages, liability for possible damage done, loss of working card, forfeiture of trade union, housing, or other privileges, fine, durance. Those in charge of production operations likewise have stern duties to perform; manufacture of poor goods, or too slow manufacture in general, is regarded as a crime against the state. For an accident occurring to a railway train those in charge may be criminally liable.

Provision is made for the adjustment or settling of labor disputes or disagreements; and workers are supposed to abide by the decisions rendered. Under the circumstances strikes are seldom to be expected. Any engaged in procuring or fomenting them might readily be accused of "counter revolution." After a strike is over its leaders may be duly disposed of. For permitting such conditions as may lead to strikes, labor unions and state officials may be charged with dereliction in the performance of their duties.

There are factory councils and committees concerned with economic considerations, with cultural matters, and above all with increased production. As might be expected, production has been held back from time to time by what can only be designated as factory debating societies or by drawn-out committee deliberations. Workers in factories are permitted to make suggestions as to their management and operations—a procedure that works two ways, good and bad.

All in all, things economic have not gone very well in Soviet Russia, and the economic dreams of the promoters of its policies have been far from coming true—though in all fairness it must be said that whatever unfavorable results there have been are not to be laid wholly at the door of its peculiar economic organization.

Apart from what has happened in the struggles with the peasant farmer, industry cannot be said to have fared altogether happily in the land. Production has been much below what is needed for a country the size of Russia; distribution has been in a greater or less state of uncertainty and disorder; the quality of goods offered has seldom been of a high order, and often quite poor; and the prices charged have been frequently exorbitant. The railway system has been inadequate, and has been overtaxed. Train service has not always been reliable. Railway traffic has often been crowded and congested at various points; goods have been moved slowly and clumsily. Roads over the country are for the most part poor, and not too many of any kind, with little automobile travel outside the cities. Standards of living have remained low. The masses have been in pitiful need of consumer goods. (Rationing has been known even in times of peace.) Methods of advancing industry have not infrequently been crude and ill-digested. Some industries have been badly integrated. Parts of machinery in factories have at times been poor, defective, or unsuited. Some factories have been unable to get raw material when needed. There has been much waste of material. There has been much breaking down and wearing out of machinery; it has often deteriorated rapidly. Goods have been spoiled in manufacture. Nor can charges of sabotage by internal enemies explain all the shortcomings and flounderings. High costs and ineffi-

ciency of operations have often been caused, on the one
hand, by confused, disorganized, muddled, garrulous
mass or "committee" direction, and, on the other hand, by
an interfering and dominating government bureaucracy.
Lack of expert guidance and direction has sometimes been
painfully in evidence. Even the production of food has at
times been below what we might expect; food shortages,
even famines, have not been unknown.

Under all the circumstances there was bound to be some
confusion and disarray. The country has been undergoing
the pains of a new industrial order—a country that has
hardly been prepared or qualified to carry on large industrial undertakings. The task of making Soviet Russia
into a great industrial nation could not be expected to be
an easy one. New types of machinery have been put into
use not before known in the land. Workmen lacked
mechanical competency. An industrialization which usually
requires a space of many years was to be rushed through
in the space of a few. The country has stumbled and
groped forward toward industrialization. Perhaps credit
is to be bestowed chiefly when consideration is taken of
the depth from which it has had to come. With the years
general industrial efficiency in Soviet Russia has on the
whole increased, however slowly.

In the industrial development of Soviet Russia there
has been forced labor on a gigantic scale—to an extent
that may only be surmised. The fact is that on account of
the vast amount of work, including the schemes of public
work, to be carried on in that land (not omitting the immense exertions in the making of war supplies and muni-
tions), there are not enough workers available; no small
part of the population has to be drafted. Furthermore,
because of the inexpertness or heavy-handedness in the
more or less technical operations, together with the lack
of sufficient modern equipment, several laborers are re-

quired to do what one could do in a country like the United States. In a sense, also, all labor is in large part of compulsory character. The state excuses no one, and may assign to labor much as it sees fit, whether in the factory, on the farm, or elsewhere, although such transfer of labor may often be referred to as "voluntary" on the part of the worker. Most employees are engaged at allotted tasks, or at whatever is offered them, perhaps regardless of preparation or qualifications; should they balk, they stand to lose membership in trade unions, insurance benefits, and certain civil rights, and to have their names removed from labor exchanges. For persons of specified ages compulsory labor is provided for by law. Under the circumstances there need be little unemployment in the land.

Though in the future a greater force of laborers may be available to the state through the results of a high birth rate, it is possible at the present to augment the number, or to prevent the exhaustion of a normal labor supply, or to create a labor reserve. Women may be called upon to do various forms of work, some quite onerous, though this is something to which Russian women have long been inured. Advantage may also be taken of the provisions of the law as to apprentice work for children and youth; these provisions may at times be stretched, especially by mass training for a short period, to permit regular manual tasks. Further labor force is in political offenders.

Workers are theoretically free to move about over the land; but there is in reality no great mobility of labor. Workers must keep record books with them, constituting a sort of internal passports. This impedes their movements; it may tie them down to factory or farm, and prevent their seeking new jobs. There has, in fact, been considerable labor turn-over in the country, and considerable wandering about of would-be workers. It has been regarded necessary to put a curb on these migratory tendencies, especially on the part of rural workers desirous of trying their fortunes in the already overcrowded cities, a curb perhaps to be accomplished by the withholding of passports.

In general there can be said to be real exploitation of the workers in Soviet Russia; they are under the one employer possible to them—as a rule they can have no other master.

Regimentation of labor has been carried on with a rod of iron, and with a heart of stone. There are no official records to indicate the hardships and inhumanities that have been inflicted, especially in the liquidation of what has run counter to Soviet economic policy.

Wages paid in Soviet Russia are higher than they were in Czaristic Russia. This circumstance is, however, more than counterbalanced by the higher costs of living today —without allowance for the several forms of state aid to workers, or the several forms of economic insurance (accident, health, unemployment, old age), besides shorter work days (except when war orders are pressing), vacations with pay, and admission to rest homes and sanatoria.

Wages paid to the workers in Soviet Russia are an uncertain quantity; they involve elements and factors peculiar to Soviet ways and processes of reasoning, and perhaps a bit bewildering to the outsider.

The preferred method of work in industrial establishments is piece work. The wage here may be increased by extra payments or rewards for special efficiency or for acceleration of production. By the Soviet people it is claimed that the various public services rendered by the state (medical treatment, education, recreation facilities, etc.) are to be regarded as supplementing wages; though such a conception of "socialized wages" as a ground for the paying of reduced wages would have little acceptance in capitalist countries. For some groups in the population, especially those on the farms, security through social insurance measures is less available than for other groups. It is not always easy, in addition, to ascertain how fully or how promptly claims in this respect are met. The situation is further complicated by the circumstance that prices charged over the country are not always the same. They may vary at different stores. Rent, all things considered, comes nearest to reasonable figures. In comparison with the days before the Soviets came to power, intellectual and professional workers are in general much worse off, something to which the Soviet state would not be expected to be altogether averse. Probably persons like writers or artists fare best. There is more or less price fixing.

There are conflicting stories that come out of Russia as to what the workers actually receive for their work. It is far from easy to determine just what are "real wages" (measured by the extent and character of the goods to be purchased from earnings). Soviet claims are said to be misleading and confusing. Whatever, moreover, may be obtained as earnings, there are reports of inflated or fantastically high prices which have to be paid for consumer goods. According to this measurement wages are said to be not much more than a pittance. (Some of the Soviet factories are asserted to have been built at starvation wages.) At all events we can have few doubts that even if standards of living are above those maintained in pre-Soviet days, they are appreciably below those in most capitalist countries. The main question is whether this must necessarily be the case, or whether changes are possible.

In the wages or salaries paid to workers a dead levelism does not exist; nor is any pretense made that it does. In no inconsiderable degree are there gradations of income among citizens. Payment for work may be determined by the quantity and the quality of the work done, or by the

measure of skill and experience of the individual worker,
as well as by the contribution of each to what is regarded
as the social value of the article produced, or by general
social considerations. Piece work rates, bonuses for special industrial assiduity, and the introduction of labor-
saving machinery may all find justification in the conviction that greater production for the community as a
whole is thereby achieved. Agricultural distribution may
even be according to the work done by each worker. All
this is looked upon as common sense, at least at the present juncture, and not in violation of any fundamental
socialist doctrine. Excessive salaries are paid to none.

Rewards of industry may be expressed otherwise than
in monetary returns. For those in possession of needed
skill in the economic endeavors of the state, or for those
with marked ability in directing industry, or for those
displaying superior workmanship therein, there may be
recompense of more or less tangible nature, though not
in the coin of the realm. To such persons, or to favored
or privileged groups in general, certain perquisites are
possible. There may be access to better or lower-priced
stores or restaurants, assigning of more comfortable or
more convenient dwelling apartments, prompter and better
medical service, more pleasant or somewhat speedier railway traveling, more or less occasional use of state automobiles, more desirable seats at the opera or play,
more expeditious recourse to sanatoria or rest homes or
claim to better accommodations therein, and so on. It is
the government functionary or holder of office who usually comes off best in these respects. On the other hand,
dilatory, supine, lackadaisical workers, or slackers, or
those who do not manifest sufficient zeal or eagerness in
the operations of labor unions or coöperative associations
may find themselves in disfavor or discriminated against
in one way or another.

In the economic life of Soviet Russia there is one phase that is of idyllic nature. There is preached, and to a greater or less extent practiced, a principle of mutual help or of voluntary, unpaid labor for the cause. Notably meritorious or outstanding services or activities in industrial operations are requited by public recognition or honorable mention. This industrial public-spiritedness or social emulation may be manifested in one of several forms. Upon men (and women) who produce more than was expected of them or more than others, or who have broken records in production, or who have shown superior skill or aptitude, or who have brought to light improved methods of production, or who have made the earliest delivery of products, or who have displayed the highest degree of coöperation, or who have the best balance sheet—upon these is bestowed the benediction of the state. To factories in front there may be prizes or awards. There may also be "wall newspapers," upon which are rolls of honor for those who have performed extraordinarily well—and possibly corresponding rolls of dishonor.

Appeal may be made to the sporting instinct, or to the spirit of competitive sportsmanship—in a new kind of game or play. Factory, farm, or office groups may be pitted against each other to see which can accomplish the most. Thereupon the winning team may go over to the losing and find out what the trouble is, point out shortcomings and defects, and show the way to improvement, lending perhaps not only advice but direct manual assistance—all for the weaker sisters who have not done so well. Shock brigades may take it upon themselves to make up some shortage in the industrial structure, on the farm, in the factory, or on the traffic ways, or to meet some emergency therein, giving without cost their time and energy. Holidays may be surrendered to make sure that a particular task is moved toward completion in the interest of the state.

Very efficient workers are not only publicly extolled; they are sent from place to place to inspire other workers by precept and example, constituting a sort of "pep squad" to stimulate to ever greater exertion—to stress the importance of increased production and to proclaim and expound the doctrines of communism in general.

Finally, toward labor a new attitude is taken. Its dignity becomes no idle abstraction. Labor is not to be regarded as drudgery on the part of an inferior, but something to be shared by all, in honor and in joy, and in service for the community.

Such is the shining picture, such the thrilling story that has come to us out of Utopia. So far as there is recognition of things so fine and admirable in the daily doings of men anywhere on this earth, we can only bestow our blessings upon their heads. With respect to Soviet Russia, before we can commend them to the rest of the world, we shall feel entitled to hear much more about them; we shall want to know more of their spontaneity, their artlessness, their penetration, their breadth, their persistence. Just how far is this intensification of labor, this form of pace-setting, of speeding up, a government scheme for increasing production? Just how far does there exist inward compulsion from the state? And are not those who engineer these ventures motivated by some more or less material reward? But in any event Soviet Russia deserves well at our hands for having given us the conception that some of these things are worth thinking about in an industrial state.

How far the economic outcome in general in Soviet Russia is to be ascribed to inherent efficiency or inefficiency of state socialism, or to the kind that has shown itself there, or to the character and condition of the country in which it has been essayed, or to circumstances not entirely propitious for its introduction and continuance, there is none as yet to tell us. Even if the land was good soil for the trying out of socialism, there should have been a much longer time for preparation. It must always be remembered that there has been involved a gigantic attempt to transform a backward agrarian state into a modern industrial one, and one largely standing aloof in its policies and practices from other nations.

CHAPTER IX

EDUCATION IN THE SOVIET STATE

NO LESS pronounced than the economic revolution that has taken place in Soviet Russia has been the cultural. One of the most hopeful and yet one of the most disturbing things in the whole Soviet undertaking has lain in the system of education that has been instituted there. This has to do both with the vast amount of illiteracy that has existed in Russian territory and with the purposes and methods of instruction that have been pursued.

The problem of illiteracy or of extremely limited or of the barest education, inherited as it has been from the old Czaristic régime, has been of a seriousness which it is difficult to exaggerate. It may be said with a large measure of truth that from the situation as to education all of the troubles of old and of present Russia have had their origin. It cannot be repeated too often that the Russian people, with all their noble and generous qualities, have been for years upon years sunk in a mire of illiteracy, that whatever education has been afforded them has been of the most restricted and elementary character, and that the knowledge of the masses of the people with regard to the great world outside their borders, or even of distant parts of their own land, was hardly to be counted.

In such circumstances, with a vast portion of an immense population singularly backward in education, with enormous distances separating people, with roads poor and often all but impassable, the wiping out of illiteracy and the creation of an educated citizenry becomes a gigantic task—gigantic enough for the most intelligent and the most progressive government, and for the ablest educational generalship of the world, supplied with abundant financial resources, manned with the most skilled teaching force, and with a program extending over a long period of years.

Be it said to the high credit of the Soviet government that it has been alive to the seriousness of its problem, and has never wearied in bringing it to public attention. It has been doing far, far more in the way of attack than was ever the case under the old Czaristic régime—which in fact did almost nothing. There has been awakened a genuine and far-reaching thirst for knowledge. In a sense education may be said to have become a passion in the land. The "liquidation" of illiteracy is the alluring slogan for its doing away with. In the inviting campaign are marshalled all classes. Each of the organizations in the Soviet network has a place in the heated program. Without a modicum of education soldiers may not leave the army. Ready means of instruction for all the people are at hand in such vehicles as the radio, the motion picture, the public billboard, the museum. We are being treated to the spectacle of a nation rising in massed attack upon its ancient foe. It is doubtful if ever in the world's history there has been presented such a drama, or if there has been so great a tribute to education.

In its general educational policies the Soviet government has faced in one respect a relatively easy and simple task. As with everything else that has come into its hands, it has had quite a clean slate to work upon, with no left-over ways or measures to clog or impede the operations of its own plans, with no traditions or ancient customs to get rid of, with no opposition or critical element to put obstacles in its path or to find serious fault. Whether its principles and procedure be good or not, the Soviet government has had a rare opportunity to put into practice the latest theories or ideas in education, and to avail itself of the latest expert pronouncements upon the subject. No nation has ever been given, at least in modern times, such *carte blanche* as to what it shall do in the instruction of its children. Russia might have provided a vast educational laboratory for the enlightenment of the rest of the world, though in not a few respects that country is hardly the fittest one for such experiments.

As compared with the countries of western Europe and the United States, educational standards in the U.S.S.R. are not in general to be regarded as of the highest. For the most part in what we call "pure" education it falls short of the levels reached in those countries.

Schools in this socialist commonwealth may be established not only in cities, towns, and villages, but in connection with or as appurtenance to a factory or farm. Higher education is mostly under the aegis of the central state government, with lower forms largely entrusted to political subdivisions or to local units, always with more or less supervision from the general authorities.

The child in Soviet Russia begins his education at a very early age; in fact he steps into it from the nursery— or rather he may in these years be said to have one foot in the nursery and one in the school. (Formally the first three years are in the crèche, the next four in the kindergarten—under the health and education authorities, respectively.) A more or less incidental result of this early start in education is to dilute the allegiance the child owes to the parent and to turn more of it to the state—to weaken the influence of the home in the building of the child's life and character, and to vest more of these things in the control of the state.

The educational process is of an advanced order and follows the most advanced theories. On one hand and on another it has shown opposition or reaction to what it has been pleased to call formalism in education. The guiding principle in the school is self-expression on the part of the child. The much-loved committee concept of the Soviet people reaches even to children in the schools; they are to have a word to say, along with their teacher, as to what and how and by whom they are to be taught. The child is to observe, to question, to judge for himself. He is to learn by doing. Dramatics, drawing, music, with the museum, have no small place in the educational process. Schooling is designed as a laboratory matter, within and without the classroom. Nor must it be forgotten what the country is and stands for. From childish throats shrill chants of praise to the "Red" Commonwealth in which they joyously dwell; to children in less favored lands are stretched childish hands of sympathy. In Soviet teaching about other lands there is not always the strictest adherence to the truth.

A notable feature in instruction is the combination or correlation of vocational education with cultural education. Schools are semi-technical institutions, manual labor and intellectual instruction going hand in hand, or linked together in striking fashion. To play is given a utilitarian side. It may include instruction in making useful things or employment at useful toil. Toys may be in the guise of tools, models, mechanical devices, all designed to lead to later creative labor or to other occupation that will be of advantage to the state. Technical education has received paramount attention. Because of the returns that are to be expected in public service, government subsidies to higher and to technical education are relatively large. Promising students are encouraged to go through college or technical school; workers, to learn more for their advancement. But education in terms of material value is not all. Physical education has a high place; elementary hygiene has a definite niche. Not seldom are opportunities seized upon to give lessons in such matters as sanitation to children, and to their elders as well.

Adult education, also largely of vocational or utilitarian character, receives hardly less consideration. Technical and agricultural institutes may be set up in different places for workers, with a greater or less amount of their time devoted to the purpose. In the factory, on the farm, in the trade union, in the club, education in some form may continue.

Matters as to education in Soviet Russia are made the worse by the attitude or peculiar slant toward it. Education as set forth by the authorities of that country is, strictly speaking, hardly education at all; it is made a political thing. In the Soviet scheme of education, what is so denominated is in large degree primarily and fundamentally the inculcation of particular propaganda or the moulding into a particular pattern. The propaganda here, it is true, happens to be communism, but in the long view of the matter this is rather a detail, and does not affect the general principle—though the Soviet authorities would say quite differently. In the whole undertaking are adopted dogmatic attitudes—though if such should show their heads among peoples having contrary views, they would meet bitter denunciation.

Besides the formal means of education in the schools for the inculcation of communistic principles, there are other agencies set up for political instruction and indoctrination, and of a peculiarly Soviet order. The Communist party is not content with having adults in its councils or among those who are to be moulded by its direction. To have a firm and complete grip upon the entire population, it turns to account its younger elements, proceeding to ever lower levels, and finally to the foot of the ladder of life. It organizes in efficient battalions its youth, its children, and almost its infants. For those of high school, college, or professional school age, there is the Young Communist League, in preparation for membership in the Communist party itself, and which is very active in services to it. Below it and ready in time to pass into it are the Young Pioneers of grammar school age, performing tasks like those of the Boy Scouts of America, but with a most communistic leaning and color. At the bottom are those of elementary and kindergarten age, who bear the significant Soviet title of Octobrists, and who in their baby ways find communistic work to do.

In education is not included knowledge of the outside world—its activities and opinions. As to this the people are kept in heavy darkness, getting only what the government wants them to get. Nor is there always full knowledge of what goes on in the Soviet land. With all its zeal for education, Soviet Russia does not let its people know all—something that betrays a want of complete faith in education, and something also that does not savor of complete honesty.

Perhaps education has proceeded at too fast a pace. Like so many other things in Soviet land, it gives one the impression that there is something superficial, something a bit unreal, about it.

Education in Soviet Russia goes far beyond the schoolroom. In a sense the whole population is seething with the new-found thing. Desire for knowledge has swept up and down the land. Printed matter of all kinds has poured from the presses. Newspapers find avid perusers. There are new books, and new readers for them. In many workers' clubs, which occupy so prominent a place in the life of the country, reading rooms are a necessary adjunct. There are museums—educational, scientific, agricultural, industrial. There are excursions and tours. Local libraries are encouraged—perhaps local "Chautauquas" with study

courses, lectures, concerts, and so on. In bringing education and intellectual activity to some backward (and more
or less bewildered) national groups in the vast Soviet
territory, it has been necessary to provide an alphabet or
a grammar. No known medium is neglected in educating
the masses—or perhaps in spreading communistic dogma.
(There are museums appertaining to the "revolution.")
Nothing may be uttered or printed or otherwise dissem-
inated that does not have the imprimatur of the authorities.
To all forms of education must there be a communist
approach.

Education is not merely a means of dealing with youth;
through it as a universal force man is to be made over—
that is, into a good communist, with all that communism
signifies. Soviet Russia has been educationally engaged in
nothing less than the most stupendous and ambitious program ever undertaken by a nation.

Public discussion follows in the wake of the new and
wide concern with education. It is now a national pastime;
with it there is almost constant mass instruction in civics,
or in the affairs of the Soviet state. The pointing out of
public abuses or evils, or a sort of state self-criticism,
is an indulgence vivaciously participated in by all. Our
commendation of this nation-wide public forum is tempered by the consideration that in it there must be nothing
beyond what is prescribed by the government. There may
be finding of fault with details, but never with the system.
The only public opinion permitted is the official one.

Newspapers, be it said to their credit, do not stress personal crimes or scandals, unless the state should in some
way be concerned. Not a little space, it is also to be
acknowledged, is devoted to scientific and cultural discus-
sions, and to more and better industrial production. Citizens are encouraged to criticise internal policies or arrange-
ments or ventures, which they do sometimes in a sharp or

severe vein. On the other hand, there may be all but complete silence as to a serious railway wreck or a devastating famine. Foreign news is often of misleading character, perhaps distorted or with exaggeration of unfavorable events or circumstances. Newspapers serve chiefly or largely as purveyors of government propaganda. They are to a greater or less extent mouthpieces of the state—or shall we say of the Communist party?

Whether or not the result of a sort of frenzy over the new education or over the general blessings manifest in the Soviet state, there are, in both the country and the city, unceasing meetings, speeches, processions.

With all this there is continual adulation, a sort of public ballyhoo, in regard to the potentialities and the achievements of the Soviet state. There are grandiloquent boasts and claims. No opportunity is passed by for boosting, and for proclaiming as the "biggest" or the "grandest" this or that enterprise of the state. Perhaps attention is called to the wickedness of the outside world which has the temerity or the ignorance to question or to belittle or to find fault. Everywhere are depicted or emblazoned the shortcomings and the horrors of the capitalistic state, and the virtues, advantages, and glories of the socialistic—on billboards, in cartoons, in art galleries, in theaters, over loud-speakers. The drabness of much of the Soviet undertaking is made up for in some degree by the glamorous descriptions with which it is invested.

Scientific research is sponsored on a far-reaching scale, and not infrequently in high-sounding language. There have been created endless institutes—of chemistry, biology, physics, agriculture, genetics, archaeology, literature, aviation, electricity, medicine, machine building, promotion of workers' welfare—agriculture alone having a wide variety. Whatever the depth of the foundation, there is a certain furore over science in the land. Popular participation in it is encouraged, for its own sake and for what it can do for the country. To scientists making contributions of notable worth may be given prizes or emoluments. The incitement of scientific experimentation and exploration on the part of the Soviet government has in some fields won the gratitude of the world. Long will be acclaimed the epic that had its seat in the frozen Arctic. But the world does not forget that scientific research (if dealing with matters appertaining to socialism) cannot always be expected to be strictly objective, or "pure"; it may here be given the hue that the Soviet state wishes it to have. Censorship and propaganda even in the holy realm of science are not asleep.

CHAPTER X

GENERAL CULTURE AND MATERIAL
WELL-BEING

IN THE field of art, whether in the sphere of education or of general culture, the Soviet government has another claim to our respect and admiration. Art in its broadest and fullest sense is being preserved in Soviet Russia in a highly creditable manner—"preserved," for art has always had a high place in Russian life, and Soviet Russia is but holding up the national traditions. Not only collections of art, but places of historic interest are made available for all the people, who are encouraged to visit and enjoy them. The priceless collections at the Winter Palace and the Hermitage in Leningrad, and at the various institutions maintained in Moscow and in other cities, as well as numerous museums in all the larger cities, attest the appreciation of this form of education or of art on the part of the Soviet government. For its work of preservation and care of historical and archaeological monuments in general it deserves the thanks of lovers of art, of culture, of history the world over. Encouragement is given to native arts and crafts. Nor must mention be omitted of endeavors in city planning or of attempts to combine beauty with utility in the rebuilding of the land. In certain of the cities, notably Moscow, where towering modern structures touch elbows with quaint reminders of far-gone days, narrow ancient lanes may emerge into lovely spacious vistas or garden-like squares, lined with goodly trees or arrayed with flowers. And it is Moscow's subway, or Metro, which declares that none other in the world has been constructed with so much attention to what is pleasing to the eye.

In dramatic production also the Soviet government is living up to the conceptions and performances of old Russia. Much of this is maintained in splendid fashion. Not often elsewhere is the stage of such order; and not often elsewhere are skill and labor and money so freely lavished to attain lofty standards. Excellence of execution, efficiency of technique, gorgeousness of display, cleverness of movement, all shine forth in undiminished brilliance in present Russia. This, however, is not altogether the doing of Soviet Russia; it is in part the doing of the Russian people, unchanged here whether under Czar or under Communism.

But much more is being done for art. It is not for exclusive, aristocratic circles only, but something in which all the people can share. It is democratized, made accessible to every one. No small efforts have been put forth to bring culture to the masses, and to make them in some degree appreciative. Special encouragement may be given to artists showing promise. There may be attempts at a revival of a national culture in folklore or in folk dances; for city factories or rural farms there may be encouragement of orchestras; for different industrial or other groups festivals may from time to time be organized. By trade unions, coöperative associations, and other Soviet organizations is culture promoted.

In the matter of culture, however—an expression so freely used in Soviet Russia—some of the finer values that have been associated with the term are lost. In the use of high-sounding phrases, in which the Soviet state excels, probably no term is so overworked or so abused as is the term "culture." Under it is covered a multitude of matters, some rather pertaining to personal etiquette. In addition, in the promotion and development of that consideration, the only agency is the state. It remains the arbiter in determining what is and what is not to be regarded as cultural. As everywhere else, no culture is permitted that might bring harm to the communist cause.

Let it be said also to the credit of the Soviet state that it is endeavoring to provide recreation and entertainment for all its people. Remote villages may now be brought within the reach of the motion picture or other form of diversion. The abounding "parks of rest and culture" have appeal for all classes from Coney Island roller coasters and circuses to all manner of games (not excluding games like chess), folk dances, festivals, lectures, concerts, art exhibits. The activities of a workers' club read like those of a social settlement or a paternalistic welfare program in America. In profuse array throughout the land thrive sports, athletics, physical culture activities. Clubs for such purposes are almost everywhere. Sport clubs are promoted by trade unions and other organizations, perhaps as part of their work. By many industrial establishments facilities are provided for sports or physical culture.

The activities that can come under the name of "sport" are more or less state-planned and state-directed. There is not much room or opportunity for the play of private initiative or enterprise. "Clubs" for sport, for entertainment, for culture, for young and for old, which swarm over the land, and which may nominally be "private," tell the tale: behind the scenes is the Soviet *deus ex machina*. What are called "voluntary" committees or other organizations may manifest a concern or take some action with regard to this matter or that; they may go about the community or from place to place, in the interest of better health, better education, or better something else, conducting campaigns, and if necessary holding public meetings.

But there is little of which the government does not know and does not approve. "Private" organizations must be duly registered. Toleration of those that might be antagonistic to or subversive of the Soviet régime could hardly be expected. Should "private" meetings be too frequent or with too large an attendance, the matter would soon reach the attention of the authorities. In Soviet land nearly everything is prepared for the individual citizen; almost all is overorganized. There is virtually nothing in the lives of the men and women of the country that does not suffer regimentation in greater or less degree—culture, sport, education, industry, one's very life. Some enjoy it, in a sort of childish glee; others find it onerous or tedious or wearisome. Some heartily approve.

In sport as well as in other state activities stress is placed upon physical culture. Health examinations, proper exercise, instruction in the building up of able-bodied, sturdy, robust citizens have been no small part of the Soviet program—in some respects almost to the point of worship—though possibly in actual results with little more achieved than in certain other countries of the world. The land teems with youth movements, abounding in energy and enthusiasm, all with their "strength through joy." Young workers are to have "healthy lungs, strong muscles, steady nerves, sound hearts"—something to which youth might aspire in all lands. The health of the people is regarded as necessary for the welfare of the state.

In Soviet Russia there have been praiseworthy, if not the most deep-seated, efforts to cope with disease—in a country where such efforts had long been desperately needed. A great problem in general public sanitation was found in respect to a country never known for its cleanliness—a problem far from being solved still. Broad programs have been set on foot, including a popular educational campaign through lectures, exhibits, posters, pamphlets. The illness of one is declared to be the concern of all; and prevention is to have foremost regard. There is a network of more or less interrelated organizations—so dear to the Soviet heart. Its medical and public health vocabulary overflows with such terms as prophylactic and epidemiological institutes, medical centers, health stations, medical supplies industries, sanitariums, maternity homes, laboratories, sanitation centers, clinics, hospitals, dispensaries, first aid, polyclinics, health resorts, medico-therapeutic facilities, health museums, scientific research, nurseries, child health centers.

Medical treatment of some kind is to be made available for the entire population as far as possible, and extending into rural areas. There are health centers in many cities and towns and in many of the larger industrial establishments; roving physicians or traveling clinics go about the country, and free medical services are given through some form of state insurance. Medical treatment, in keeping with general socialist principles, is in no small measure of institutional character. Some hospitals are quite up-to-date, with modern equipment. Great medical skill, approaching that of the countries of Western Europe, can hardly be expected. It is good to be able to say that on the way out are the medical fakers, soothsayers, and witch doctors which have infested the land.

Care and treatment of the defective classes are not given the prominence that is the case with other matters. Mental disturbance or derangement is believed to be due largely to economic environment or to economic organization. Through economic readjustments mental readjustments are to a considerable extent to be achieved. Rest homes are to help more or less. General institutional care has some place in the program, though not a large one. It is mostly for acute cases. Psychiatric examinations are encouraged.

The treatment of classes like the blind and deaf-mutes, following, as might be expected, the form or mould of communistic Russia, is not of a particularly enlightened order. Social welfare measures as a general thing are not on a level with those of the most advanced countries of Europe, though in most respects ahead of those of old Russia. The trained social worker, as known in the United States, has made an appearance only to a very limited extent. Probably what comes nearest to organized "social work" is that done through clubs or trade unions. Social work of a sort is to be found in hospitals, prisons, nurseries, clinics, etc. There are few really trained nurses.

The birth rate in Russia has for the most part been high, in some parts the highest among the Caucasian peoples, and at times approaching what has been regarded as the maximum for the human race (which was also true of old Russia). It is about twice as high as in some other white countries. A high birth rate is favored and encouraged by the government; a material factor to this end lies in the bounties offered to families with a large number of children. It is to be remembered no less that at times the death rate has been very high. This matter has been influenced in some measure by the massed killings of a portion of the population either directly or indirectly, through abuse or mistreatment. Of more recent years mortality rates on the whole show a decline. There have been appreciable reductions in the death rate from such affections as tuberculosis, venereal disease, smallpox, and malaria, and also in the infant mortality rate. In Soviet Russia population has steadily increased, sometimes at the rate of several million a year.

In criminal proceeding justice is supposed to move simply and with celerity. Not infrequently, however, it is held up by various incidents in or out of the court room,

including certain "confessions" of which the outside world
hears at times with amazement or amusement or grief.

As a rule there are few formalities and technicalities in
legal procedure and little drawn-out litigation. In the
lower courts, along with the regular judges are "lay
judges," or a sort of jurors from the panel, chosen by the
workers. Judgments are rendered, not so much according
to legal precedents, as according to the general sagacity
and the predilections, including the communistic predilections, of the judges. Private litigation is, because of the
relatively little private business in the land, of no great
moment.

In the treatment of the criminal, Soviet Russia has had
an advanced penological program, all of which will prove
of interest, and some of which will prove enlightening, to
the rest of the world. A high place is given to what corre-
sponds elsewhere to probation or parole. Besides the old
prison structures inherited from the Czar, there are penal,
or rather correctional, institutions which are much on the
order of reformatory colonies. Imprisonment may in part
be characterized by absence of restraints or restrictions
except during hours of labor; if possible without absence
from one's family. Self-government is encouraged, recreation facilities provided, occupations with pay afforded—
perhaps with occasional vacations. In dealing with the
problem of alcohol, main recourse is to education—especially in the ridiculing of the drunkard—besides medical
attempts at cure. In measures for the treatment of the
offender in general the declared object is his reclamation;
what is aimed at is the "cure" of a "sick" man. The maximum prison term is ten years. Hopeless criminals may in
some way be eliminated.

Like so many things in the Soviet state, crime is believed
to be largely, if not solely, of economic causation. The
"punishment" concept is not supposed to be present—

except in the case of political offenders, who may receive punishment of the most abhorrent kind, even worse than in Czaristic days. Stealing of property from the state is a more heinous thing than stealing it from the individual. Crime to a considerable extent, in fact, is defined as the "undermining" or "weakening" or "overthrow" of the economic functions or of the power and authority or general administration of the state, perhaps under the name of "counter-revolution." Capital punishment is reserved for those who endanger the social order—that is, communism.

Housing construction, of which there has been a prodigious amount in Soviet days, has too often been of a cheap or flimsy character. In the cities the trend is toward large-scale apartments, rather than individual homes, the better to promote communal living. Apartment overcrowding and room overcrowding still constitute a serious problem. Complaint is sometimes made that much of the money that goes into club structures and facilities could be put to better use in providing family dwellings. With the birth rate high, and with migrants from the country pouring into the cities, it may not be easy to catch up on the housing situation. Inadequate housing and poor housing may long continue. The matter is not helped much by the persistent creation of new cities. Homes, especially those of an apartment nature, are largely constructed by the state (perhaps through municipalities), with some by industrial establishments for their employees, and with not a little through coöperative bodies; there is encouragement of the building of small individual homes by those who are to live in them, possibly with greater or less state aid.

In the matter of the family, or in the regulations as to marriage and divorce Soviet Russia has gone far. The earlier laws permitted marriages to be effected merely by

registration at some government bureau of the couple concerned, with perhaps a witness; qualifications were few;
few questions were asked. When either party became
weary of the marital relation, or perhaps when a new
union was sought, little was called for beyond a similar
registration with a small fee, a postcard notice to the other
spouse, and all was off. Some citizens have been able to
point to a considerable line of ex-wives. Marriage may be
contracted not only from matrimonial desires, but with an
eye to practical utility, or for the aid the wife can render
in one's muscular tasks. Rural dwellers have at times
entered into the married state to get needed help on the
farm in a busy season; when the heavy work is over, they
could turn to divorce. The only concession that may
have been made to the supposed decencies of life was that
one spouse may have been required to make contribution
for the support of the other, with aid also for possible
children of the previous marriage. In the earlier days of
the Soviet state abortions were legalized, and were numerous. (They are permitted now only when necessary to
save the life of the mother.) Illegitimate children are of
equal legal status with legitimate. Marriages are legal
whether registered or not. The age-long problem of prosti-
tution, which according to Soviet philosophy is almost
wholly the result of economic conditions, is glibly declared
to be solved through medical treatment in special institutions of those who practice that profession and their training for jobs.

Married women are related to the state directly, and not
through any supposed partnership arising from marriage.
A wife may retain her former name, and may have a different domicile from that of her husband.

With the idea of lightening the physical labors of the
housewife, and at the same time further to sap the strength
of the individual home, there have been promoted or en-

couraged communal kitchens, dining rooms, laundries, etc., together with wide sales of ready-prepared foods. "Kitchen factories" is a term that has an established place in the Soviet vocabulary. Over half of the industrial population of the country, is said to be fed in large communal dining halls. Nor do crowded apartments have wholesome effect upon family life. A pronounced competitor of the home has also been the ubiquitous club, with its various alluring recreational and cultural features; it is often the pet of the Soviet state. The entire process is in line with the general attitude toward the family. It may be on insecure foundations and unstable; the state is to be the all in all.

In the rearing of the child the state is to have a hand and to accept responsibility to a greater or less extent— through a chain of advisory centers, milk stations, kitchens, crèches, infant nurseries, nursery schools, and kindergartens, or until the period of formal schooling is well under way. Whether engaged at work or in attendance upon some entertainment, the mother may look to some means provided by the state for the care of her child, perhaps in connection with a factory, a coöperative association, a section of a town. The mother need keep her child only a couple of months. She is not required to place it with any state agency; but if she does she has more time as a worker or a citizen. Parental control of the child is co-existent with or shared with that of the state. Punishment of the child is denied to the parent. One pathetic result of the weakening of the home and of family life was the army of children wandering over Russia in the earlier days, many of whom died, and others had to be placed in special homes or institutions or colonies (some being farmed out in private homes). These homeless children were often diseased, tough, swaggering, cunning, nimble-footed. The situation in respect to them, however, was partly ascribable to general conditions in the land after the initial war ordeals.

Though Soviet Russia, true to communistic principles, declares marriage to be a personal matter, and not within the special purview of the state authorities, there have been those, as in certain advanced circles in other lands, who have expressed something like ridicule or contempt for the institution; what have been regarded as old-fashioned notions on the subject have been satirized. In connection, furthermore, with the mass bringing up of children, and the almost immediate care of them by the state, the family, the one natural institution lying between the individual and the state, has not been looked upon as of the greatest concern; many of its functions, it is said, are being lost, and it might as well largely be done away with. Respect for it is enjoined upon neither the child nor the citizen.

In no country has the "emancipation" of women, or equality between the sexes, proceeded so far, and become so established a principle, as in Soviet Russia. Women, in a wretchedly low position in old Russia, have now been placed on a level with men legally, politically, economically, socially, culturally. (Perhaps the part played in the matter by biological laws is to be more or less an after discovery). The fact of marriage may leave a woman as free as before in her occupation, activities, interests. Not only are suffrage and office holding before her, but equal vocational training and equal entry into the industrial pursuits of the country. Not only have large numbers of women come into manual labor and professional callings, but relatively large numbers have also been engaged as technicians, in research undertakings, and in general governmental service.

The time has not come for the painting of the Soviet people in their socialist kingdom. But the fair·portrait or the handsome stories put forth by the Soviet authorities or their agencies to the outside world are, to say the least, premature; they are decidedly overdrawn, so far as they relate to present-day conditions—portraits or stories depicting a "land of hope" or "blessedness," with a happy, contented, well-dressed, well-conditioned people of all classes, in the van of which always are singing youth. There is here quite too evident the hand of the promotion engineer, the salesman who wishes to "sell." Too obvious is the desire to make a "front," to create an impression in the world without, to cover or to hide whatever there is of nakedness or of ugliness within.

Somehow one cannot rid one's self of the doubt whether the enthusiasm and the fervor reported so loudly and displayed so rapturously on behalf of the Soviet state is not just a bit a made-to-order thing, a state-concocted thing, a thing inspired by some hand within the Kremlin.

CHAPTER XI

MORAL AND RELIGIOUS ATTITUDES

In Soviet Russia not much standing is given to what are usually known as moral concepts. These are regarded as puerile, antiquated things, having little place in the irreconcilable class struggle. They are perhaps to be smiled at in the present day, especially by youth. In their stead is only what is held to be physically or hygienically desirable. Moral restraints have been lifted; there is no moral law. A "wide-openness" has tended to prevail.

If it be said that "private" morals are not worthy of formal regard, it is to be remembered that among the Russian people certain attitudes have, for a long time, not been altogether the same as in more western lands, but that among them as a whole there exists a common honesty which compares well with that of nearly all other countries. In Soviet Russia, moreover, there is a notable attitude toward public morality, or the conduct of those in public office. Here a high position is taken: there is a holding to rigid standards, at least theoretically, and to a considerable extent quite sincerely, with the enunciation of a strict, in part almost puritanical, code of behavior. Such practices as graft or corruption in government or in the offices of the state, or even the taking of tips, especially in the earlier Soviet period, have met with peculiarly stern reprobation.

A powerful factor in causing Soviet Russia to lose the sympathy and good-will of other countries, and in creating a feeling that the land is morally diseased, and not to be trusted, and one with which there should be few dealings, has been its attitude towards, and attacks upon, religion. It cannot be denied that there has been a steady, bitter, uncompromising warfare against religion, a campaign blatant and ruthless, an outspoken, militant "godlessness" actually gloried in—all more or less under the direction or sanction of the state. This has been unlike anything the world has ever previously witnessed.

In this land with its former vast structure of superstition, with some in the old church venal and illiterate (though with others high-minded and noble)—with the upper clergy politically servile and aloof from the masses, the church here in fact being the hand-maid of the old régime of Czar and nobility—and, in spots, with something bordering upon pagan magic (besides a number of strange, exotic sects existing in the land), assaults upon religion in the new Soviet order have been easy; and the Soviet authorities have not been slow to take advantage of the situation to give a blow as base as it has been powerful. What is of religious significance or bearing is removed or is belittled or demeaned. On every hand religious liberty has been impaired or denied. To the churches have come oppression and persecution. Not a few of the clergy have been banished or executed (sometimes on the charge of activities hostile to the Soviet state). Churches have been subjected to the heaviest kind of taxation. Church property has been confiscated, to be torn down or to be converted into storehouses, clubs, or museums. Churches may not be allowed to carry on charitable work or to relieve their members in distress. Attendance at church may draw down at least discrimination towards the offender. Religious literature may not be published or imported. Even when some expression of religious sentiment has been suffered, it has been made to appear that this was rather by way of indulgence to weaker elements of the population. Whatever of contempt or derision could be thrown upon religion has been thrown. A dogmatic atheism has ruled the day. There has been a systematic, organized campaign against religion. There have been anti-religious cartoons and posters, some vile and ribald. There have been anti-religious societies and anti-religious schools. There have been anti-religious museums, sometimes set up in a former religious structure. The campaign has been unfair, gross, rampant, violent—often or in part of official character or with official promotion or endorsement. The state has not even been neutral; it has quite definitely taken sides. Not in the days of the Czars was there such intolerance. What will be held against the Soviet power in all future pages of history will be its fearful, revolting endeavors to root religion out of the hearts of men.

Though religion as it has been for the most part understood among men has been looked upon as an obsolete institution, and something not worthy of respect, the Soviet state has fairly well proved that religion is, after all, something that its people cannot get along without. For that which has generally been accepted as such, there has been substituted, if not adoration of the communistic heroes, at least a trusting, confiding faith in what the communistic state can do, in more or less distant years—almost approaching a mystic exaltation. Their worship is truly that of the state. It is not less than state idolatry; before it there shall be no other gods.

Along with this is an odd, pathetic infatuation with science, or even with the machine—in part doubtless because of the novelty of these new forces in the lives of the people, or in childlike veneration thereof. (Henry Ford, the industrialist, not the capitalist, is their American hero.) Science as the all in all of life may be regarded as quite satisfactorily taking the place of what was once

known as morals or as religion. Through it salvation is to
be attained. In their ideology the Soviet people go beyond
socialism; through science in the socialistic state they are
to get full control over nature, and make it serve them;
through science and socialism in combination they are to
secure a new heaven and a new earth. In all this castle-
building there is something no doubt fantastic or grandi-
ose, but also something of wistful yearning that is touch-
ing.

CHAPTER XII

SLIGHTLY CHANGED OUTLOOKS IN THE SOVIET STATE

WITHIN more recent years there have come about changes in the social structure of Soviet Russia, changes notable and significant. The wildest radicalism seems to have spent its force; the swing to the farthest "left" seems to have passed. On the part of some, obsessed with the idea of plenary planning for a new world order, and eager for a sweeping change from the past, it is to be feared that orthodox Marxism has had to take a rather subservient rôle.

On different sides is to be observed a somewhat remarkable spectacle—or was it after all to be expected? In its rush after new things, in its eagerness to experiment upon nearly all possible occasions, in its readiness to play as with toys or baubles with some of mankind's most cherished heritages, Russia has wandered far. Some of its creations might be called not merely futuristic, but even cubistic. But a certain reaction has set in, even if not on a large scale, a reaction perhaps more or less inevitable. There is a little less ecstasy over the "Revolution" and its auguries, a little more sobering second thought.

Perhaps first comment is to be made upon the changes in nationalistic sentiments. Whether or not there is less international profession, there is certainly more regard and affection for Russia—present-day Russia and the Russia of the Czars. A fervid patriotism has been steadily rising in behalf of Russia the Fatherland. Russians are still Russians, still Slavs. The Socialist revolution, furthermore, is to a greater extent thought of as a Russian affair, at least for the immediate present; its international aspects and bearings do not now loom quite so large, whatever may be the issue in days a little more distant.

Family life is becoming a little more secure, a little more stable, though still much below western ideals. Loose marital relationships are more and more frowned upon; they are declared to be socially and politically unwise. In divorce proceedings both parties must now sign documents; notice must be given within a reasonable period of time to the other party; greater effort is made to collect contributions for support of former wife or of children, with payment of alimony harder to dodge; children are becoming a more important consideration in divorce cases —they must be provided for by one or both parents. The marriage bond is in fact tightening; life-long unions are upheld as desirable from all points of view, including that of the state.

Such return as there is to the ideal of the family is due mainly to concern aroused by the fact that there have been too many desertions, too many abortions, too many children without care. Another very important factor is the desire for a high birth rate to insure a large population for the country, and to insure a large army for its advancement and enhancement. It has also been discovered that fathers and mothers can love their children, and that children may even love their parents; and also that some families may prefer their own kitchen to a communal one. At any rate, the importance of the family as a social unit is having renewed emphasis. The family is found to be an institution and a force that cannot safely be dispensed with. This discovery was made by the people themselves. It constitutes in some respects, limited though it be, one of the finest tributes to human marriage in the history of the race.

There has also been some let-up in the noisy, ridiculing

assaults upon religion. While they are far from having died out altogether, and while deep-seated animosity and flaring impatience remain, the attacks are not the open, glaring things they once were. There is a little less jeering, a little less mockery. And there are still some faithful in the land. Religion seems hard to kill off altogether, even in Russia. Perhaps there will eventually be a remarkable vindication of religion in that land of Godlessness.

In the schools there is less of the reign of misrule— less of a succession of educational experiments upon the hapless children; there is appearing somewhat more of discipline and order and system. Perhaps there is slightly more attention given to spelling and the three "R's." Schools are now open to all, even to children of former officers of the Czar. In the army there is just a little less of "democracy," a little less of camaraderie, between officers and men, in the interests of military discipline. In amusements there is more of moderation; the school-holiday attitude is giving way just a bit to less confused conceptions of recreation and sport. The moulding of sartorial fashions to one pattern is being found not altogether in keeping with what human nature craves; in the shops there is just a little more concession to human vanity. Personal cleanliness is being discovered to have values in itself; the virtues of soap need not be foreign even to communists. There is a little more recognition in general of the amenities of life.

In the sphere of political economy, it is being seen that incomes are not wholly to be dissociated from individual earning capacity; there is slightly less insistence upon communal living or upon equal sharing as the only equitable or just system of social living. There is a certain realization that a modicum of private ownership or of control over a few local consumable products among peasant farmers does not come in amiss, but is rather a wise stroke of public policy.

All in all, there is a little less effort at propaganda for a particular cause, and a little less regimentation of the mass of men. There are fewer experimental innovations in one direction and another. There is more getting down to business, to brass tacks, in the conducting of human affairs, to more realistic thinking.

All this backward swing must not be taken too seriously; it must not be thought that the pendulum is moving otherwise than very slowly. But it does seem as if the worst of Soviet Russia's flings and frenzies and joy rides have been reached. What is now developing cannot be called "return to normalcy"; far from it. Yet some transformation, however slight, does appear to be taking place. Perhaps it is nothing else than the old story of the assertion of human nature. They are coming to do in Russia only what all mankind has been compelled to do from the beginning—to reckon with naked realities, and to learn from the endless series of human experiences. The Soviet state finds, however belatedly, or however faintly, that certain time-honored or time-proved values and principles may not be held lightly, or tossed aside as chaff or outworn substance.

Of promises of a better life in Soviet Russia there have been no end—promises of greater wealth for the state and for the individual, of an abundance of the things for creature comfort and for the enjoyment of the mind, of a fuller measure of culture and of knowledge of the arts, of play and fun, of the practical bestowals of science, of the achievements and general heritage of the human race. By a considerable portion of the population these promises are still largely believed. Among others, an increasing number, there are private doubts of their realization within any early period of time, or within any period of time that can readily be measured. Some are frankly fed up with promises, and are asking, even though not audibly, about the possibilities of fulfillment.

CHAPTER XIII

DEMOCRACY IN THE SOVIET STATE

B UT to whatever Soviet Russia may or may not have attained economically and culturally, there is one thing which it has not arrived at. This is democracy. Perhaps we should rather say that what has come about is the negation of democracy. Organized government in Soviet territory does not function in that capacity.

The secret of the power of U.S.S.R., or of the reason for its holding control so long, lies primarily in the remarkable organization that has been effected, an anomalous, ingenious scheme of government that may be said to be without counterpart in the history of the world. The conduct of affairs rests with what is known as the Communist party. This is no real "party" in the sense that that term is understood in other lands. In Russia this party represents only a small minority of the population— only a million or two out of Russia's one hundred and seventy millions. The rest of the people are unorganized and helpless before it.

The heart of the organization was originally composed of those who had gone through blood and fire in the old Czaristic struggles, "professional revolutionists" who had won a certain degree of skill therein. The organization as a whole is a highly centralized one. Party membership is an exclusive one, limited to a selected group. The chieftains or the inner circle form a carefully picked body, under iron discipline, austere, contemptuous of frivolity, zealous, devoted, perhaps personally impeccable or above reproach, perhaps of Spartan virtue. They constitute themselves "the keepers of the conscience" of the Soviet state. Members are chosen for their qualities of leadership. (First bidden are those having had some experience in industry.) Upon members is enjoined constant study of Soviet matters. They are carefully trained in their duties, which are principally education and propaganda among the people (with whatever harsher methods may at times be necessary), through which means control is to be secured and maintained—and the masses eventually moulded into the desired pattern. Representatives of the party are found, as a sort of nuclei or "cells," in all the reticulation of organizations criss-crossing over the land, and serving as tools or constituting cogs in the gigantic machine of government—trade unions, state farms, factory units, producers' associations, coöperative associations, army units, village officials, state trusts, universities, newspapers—all these thus being bound up with the party.

The organization of the party proceeds on a line fairly parallel with that of the Soviet government. Leaders or officials in one are in general leaders or officials in the other. Party captains occupy responsible economic and political posts. With key stations of the state in its hands, the party is in rare strategic position for ruling the country. A party representative might be installed at a vantage point in industry to watch proceedings; he might accompany the army to keep his eye on the officers. The government may be said to be composed of hand-picked party men; it is a sort of figurehead or marionette for the operations of the party.

Party principles and party discipline are alike strict. Woe to him who is not orthodox in his following. Expulsion looms up for inefficiency, corruption, disloyalty, breach of rules. Roving commissioners may take in hand those who do not see eye to eye with the supreme authorities; their cases are sooner or later properly disposed of—perhaps through elimination or "liquidation." Stories of party "purges," so far as they have reached the outside world, have shocked and sickened it.

The material rewards attaching to membership in the Communist party have already been indicated—members of this party holding in general the offices of the Soviet state. It is they who get the best of everything; it is they who constitute a privileged class. Apart from these perquisites, which are by no means to be lightly valued, party members have in their hands highly coveted power; nowhere else may there be such wide and sweeping exercise of power. There is also the joy of piloting a ship sailing uncharted seas under their peculiar banner. Perhaps these things may compensate in some measure for the thrill that in other lands comes from the struggle for wealth.

In some degree, any success of the Soviet government is attributable to the domination over it of the city dweller. It is he who has been so much the real ruler of Russia. It is his group that has been organized, and knows what is afoot. Over against his group has been chiefly the dull, uneducated, unorganized, scattered peasantry. Another highly important factor has been the lack of democratic traditions in the land.

For the enforcement of the edicts of the state there has been a powerful standing army, far better equipped and far more capable than that of any of the former Czars (whatever its ultimate strength, probably giving the best account of itself in defense of the homeland, as has been the wont of the Russian people). It constitutes the first charge upon the public treasury. Its life is relatively the most attractive and the most secure for the young men of Russia.

First in the order of the day to every inhabitant is the power of the state police. It is that which reigns over

Russia. The present system was forged from that of the Czar. Nowhere is one safe from its perennial (shall we say inherent or inevitable?) spy system. The eyes of the secret police are everywhere, and never sleep. Truly in that land there is none "who may not be afraid of the suspicion that flieth by day; nor of the terror by night; nor of the peril that walketh in darkness; nor of the destruction that wasteth at noonday." A primary purpose of the police is the suppression of "counter-revolution" in the land. At any hour may be expected the swooping arm of the law, a concentration camp, a holding without trial, a perfunctory court appearance with undisclosed sentence, perhaps attended with cruel and unusual punishment, perhaps ending in the cancellation of the life of the accused. The process of liquidation of internal enemies is easy, and by different stages — economic discrimination, deportation, shooting.

A special form of persecution or oppression lies in the forbidding of one to leave the country, or even a particular part of the country, which now to him becomes a sort of fortress. No country has had its border so closely guarded; perhaps some of those who would escape might not always have pretty tales to tell. Refugees at the same time coming into the land from foreign countries are generally looked upon with suspicion.

There are also reports from time to time of excesses under ...e color of bureaucratic power. Now and then ugly stories creep out of torture practiced, not only upon enemies of the state, but upon persons from whom unwilling money is to be extracted. Extension of torture to one's family has not been unknown.

In power remains an oligarchy, the elect of the Communist party, ruling in the name of the proletariat or of the working classes, holding in its grasp the reins of economic and political authority, with the police and the national army to carry out its will—a dictatorship, harsh and dogmatic, in the hands of a relatively small band, a virtually self-perpetuating caste of office holders, bolstered by an internal armed force of such might that none dare provoke it.   *108384*

Over and over the question comes: If the Soviet socialist state is so great a success, and has so heavy a popular following, why is police protection on so vast a scale called for in respect to political matters?

In such a country as this an expression of the will of the people is out of the question. There can be little ascertainment of the will of the majority. All who vote must vote the regular "ticket," if they know what is good for them. Definitely barred from suffrage at the outset were hirers of labor for profit, capitalists (depending on income not received from labor), merchants and traders, clergymen, the aristocracy, the landed gentry, officers of the old Czarist government and armies, certain criminals, and the mentally affected.

Even an expression of opinion contrary to the wishes of those in authority is impossible. In the old days, before the Revolution, things were not this bad. In the time of the Duma especially there was a certain measure of electoral freedom, and there was afforded a place for the expression of grievances and protests. Newspaper editors might have to exercise a degree of caution in their comments upon the activities of government; but they were not called upon to extol it. In general matters they were allowed a larger measure of liberty. Today pronouncements contrary to the views of those in power are nothing less than corruption or disloyalty or betrayal of the state. Here as well as elsewhere, toward those in position of authority there may be servile, fulsome adulation, a groveling sycophancy.

Just after the Revolution, and again a few years later, a preliminary or tentative constitution was promulgated by the Soviet inner circle. After the lapse of a score of years, during which period the people of Russia were presumed to have had a due period of tutelage and discipline, and when full-blown socialism was supposed to have arrived, the powers that be have seen fit to entrust them with a new constitution, which may or may not be a momentous event in the history of the country, and which may or may not be a step in advance or toward democracy, though indeed a striking tribute to it. (There is at least gain in the wide reading and discussion of the document.) On the whole, a slightly more liberal attitude is displayed than before.

The present constitution, a fairly elaborate instrument, may be regarded as the last word in respect to the socialist state; the modern form of the Communist Manifesto. It is the apologia, the confession of faith of communism. While set forth as the organic law of the Soviet state, it does not neglect the opportunity to proclaim the virtues of the socialist form of government, and to extol and glorify socialism. It declares that through it the "exploitation of man by man" has been destroyed. It presents a temporary version of the socialist formula: "From every man according to his ability, to every man according to his toil"—the proper phrase "according to his need" to be reintroduced when a more advanced stage of communism has been reached.

In the new constitution suffrage is universal (for all over eighteen years of age), regardless of sex, and ostensibly regardless of property holding, race, education, or present or past station in life. Balloting is asserted to be secret. As in the United States, there is a tripartite separation of powers of the government—legislative, judicial, executive. The judiciary which is established is declared to be independent. A parliament is set up in name, though an opposition, or an effective opposition, is hardly now conceivable. Provision for the Communist party does not escape reference—as a group from which candidates for office may be selected; occasion is taken to extend a eulogy upon this party which is called the "vanguard of the toilers in their struggle for the strengthening and development of the socialist order, [which] represents the directing kernel of all organizations of toilers, both public and state."

New rights of man are established—to work (with payment, which is insured by "the socialist organization of the national economy, the unceasing growth of the productive forces of the socialist party, the elimination of the possibility of economic crises, and the liquidation of unemployment"); to rest (including limitation of hours, vacations, and use of state rest homes); and economic security (with social insurance in respect to old age, illness, or incapacitation, besides free medical attention and the use of health resorts). It is not stated that the right to labor may include enforced labor—such labor as the powers that be might see fit to impose.

To education is paid a high tribute—it is to be universal, compulsory, and free (and to include higher education and education in shops, on the farm, and elsewhere). Full and equal rights (with disqualification of no kind) are given to women. Freedom of asylum, or the right of refuge, is granted, but only to those concerned "in the defense of the toilers," or in scientific activity, or in a struggle for national liberties. Rights of organizations (into various unions, industrial, cultural, etc.) are guaranteed. Tolerance toward different national or racial groups is enjoined: forbidden are any limitations to citizens because of exclusiveness or hatred on such grounds. But all such attitudes, it hardly need be stated, are in practice to be extended only when the communistic state is not thereby endangered.

Certain old freedoms are reaffirmed—but they are not absolute, and are to be exercised within restrictions believed necessary for the preservation of the socialist state.

Under freedom of the conscience, the state and the school are declared to be separate from the church; while freedom of religion is permitted, its teaching may be only in the family; freedom of "service of religious cults" is guaranteed—and so is freedom of anti-religious propaganda. Religion may not make use of the press or the radio. Freedom of speech, of the press, and of assembly (and also of public processions and demonstrations) are incorporated in the constitution; but such freedoms must be exercised "in the interests of the toilers, and with the object of strengthening the socialist system"—a circumscription that makes them of almost no value in the eyes of the rulers of the particular state.

"No humiliation of human dignity," no vengeance in punishment, the "inviolability" of the person and of the home, freedom from arbitrary arrest and from arbitrary investigations in one's home or in one's correspondence, fair and open trials for those charged with breach of the laws—such expressions or their equivalent find a place in the instrument. These are all fine-sounding phrases, but understood not to apply to political offenders or dissidents. As to the guarantee of such things as freedom of speech and of the press, world opinion will have to wait upon practical manifestations of elemental respect therefor. Soviet Russia will have to prove that it understands in any measure what civil liberty means. Men ask of what use is the secret ballot, a free press, and all the rest when the party in power holds them in the hollow of its hand, and shows no inclination of letting go. Dictatorship, officialdom can remain, constitution or no constitution. Constitutional government here has little save its trappings; democracy is hardly more than a tinkling cymbal.

Within the recesses of the Kremlin there abides a dread, uncertain power, an inscrutable force upon which the light of day does not shine. It is this which rules the land, and would rule the world.

CHAPTER XIV

THE SOVIET STATE AS A GUARANTOR OF WORLD PEACE

FROM the beginning of the Soviet state there has been disquietude and apprehension in certain quarters as to what this state might mean to the peace of the world. In its international outlook it was believed to be just possible that, conscious of the blessings to be bestowed by its rule, it might be casting covetous eyes at least upon certain nearby countries, control of parts of which would, among other things, add greatly to its strategic strength. In these lands themselves there was genuine anxiety and misgiving, and even tremor; they were never quite sure whether their taking over by Russia might not conceivably, in lieu of moral suasion, be through the exercise of more material impulsion.

The rest of the world indulged in questionings chiefly during the formative period. It was in the days of the "Revolution," and in the days just following, that there were the strongest doubts and the deepest concern lest a land dedicated to communism, convinced of the desirability of world communism, and, indeed, highly conscious of its obligations to bring about such an order with the least possible delay, might come to the decision that the surest and quickest method after all was by force of arms. But with the passage of time these fears were in great measure allayed, and were departing. It was increasingly felt that if communism was to advance and gain greater and greater possession of the earth, it was to do so by the more or less rapid conversion of the proletariat of other lands to the Soviet way of thinking, by peaceful means (including perhaps propaganda and incitement to unrest and the preparation of the soil for the seed of communism). A certain economic penetration was also possible in the importation of cheap manufactures and other goods, but not by the physical weapons of war. In international matters the world had almost come to forget Soviet perfidy in breaking with the Allies of Russia in the first World War.

The Soviet state was, furthermore, too much concerned and too much engrossed and involved in its own affairs, in the building up of its own house, to think of warring upon other lands—apart from the consideration that its very philosophy forbade any such procedure. That state made loud asseverations of its devotion to the cause and ways of peace. It would think of engaging in battle with no nation, save in the very unlikely event that its own borders were invaded and attempts made to destroy its economic and political system. However Soviet Russia was looked upon, whether it was regarded in its domestic policies with a friendly or with an unfriendly eye, the conviction grew among the peoples of the earth that it could be counted upon on the side of peace, and that the world's peace was more secure in consequence thereof. When note was taken of the part played by it in the work of the League of Nations at Geneva, there was added hope and encouragement.

The ruling powers in Soviet Russia, moreover, were believed to be anxious to preserve peace while they could build up socialism at home, they having reason to fear that war might cause great political disturbance, perhaps counter revolution; with a long peace the infiltration of socialism into other lands might be more of a possibility. Finally, the people of Russia have long been known as a pacifist people, little inclined to and little to be provoked into war, except upon strenuous instigation.

The world came to conclude that communism had at least one good thing on its side, one good thing to be said for it—its consuming hatred of war, or at any rate war that could be held as of aggressive character. It would have nothing to do therewith. It was above such an outrage upon humanity; the slaughter of human beings had no place in its program. Such things belonged to the capitalistic and the imperialistic nations, and were to be left to them.

This soothing hope and belief the nations of the earth came largely to accept. Around the world the notion crept. Peoples were in greater heart; they began to live in a high degree of assurance of the peace-mindedness of the Soviet state. That land was hailed as a powerful defender of the peace of the world. Soviet Russia, whatever its internal merits or demerits, was to contribute to peace among men.

With this attitude toward Soviet Russia on the part of the world, kindly disposed toward it in one respect at least, there came its assault upon a small, weak neighbor, an assault as brutal and ruthless as it was indefensible and unpardonable. When the time arrived, when the proper occasion arose, when it was to the advantage of the Soviet state to strike to serve its own ends, it coolly took up arms —and against an entirely innocent and unoffending, but very enlightened and progressive, nation—a nation that could not have harmed it, and would not if it could. History has not often presented anything to compare with this deed in its horror and shamelessness. The world recoiled. Nothing that Soviet Russia has or could have done has turned the world so completely from it or has alienated whatever sympathy the world had for it. By that land little has been offered by way of mitigation or exculpation beyond cries of scorn and rage directed toward those who have presumed to find fault. Its sufficient justification in its own eyes has been that it needed certain territory to make more secure its defense; no other land had any prior rights. From an invisible hand in Moscow an order came forth, telling the men of Russia to proceed to war; there was none to dissent or demur.

Puerile and vapid were the charges that the affair was to be laid at the door of Finland's "ruling classes," that Finland was a spearhead and a gateway for a long-planned attack by "capitalistic" and "imperialistic" nations (including at times even Nazi Germany), with the Soviet government acting in the nick of time, that Finland had engaged in "provocative" acts, that Finland had been "insolent" and had made a "hostile refusal" to all the Soviet's well-intentioned requests and had offered "brazen denial of facts"—charges too silly to receive credence except possibly with some of the Soviet people.

Thus has passed one of the world's delusions. It has been disheartening and saddening beyond words. The people of communistic Russia had declared that they would have nothing to do with war, at least aggressive war; they have proved that when they have their own ends to gain, they have no scruples and no hesitation in seizing upon aggressive war. Thus has come about one more disillusionment. And after all there was no reason to think that this would not be.

But more was in store for the world to learn. Upon other nearby nations Soviet Russia, under military threats, has made such demands as it may have seen fit to make, if not for territorial accessions, at least for powers over their territories, and in greater or less degree over their ways of life, that have been hardly less than direct invasion of their soil, and that have involved impairments or compromise in their sovereign rights as nations.

Even more was the world to discover. In its dealings

with weaker neighboring peoples the Soviet policy has grown ever bolder and more brazen. In bringing such lands within its orbit of control, or in more or less rapidly overcoming or subduing them, a certain technique may be said to have been developed—possibly in different stages, possibly along different lines. The orders issuing from Moscow to these lands may be more blunt or less blunt, some couched in polite-sounding diplomatic language, and some not so—but all bare-faced, and all shameless, and all charged with the spirit and tactics of the bully; not too heavily camouflaged are promises of quick, stern, and adequate military measures if compliance or obedience is not forthcoming—though attended with impudent assurances of the protection of the "safety" and "independence" of the threatened countries.

In order to gain a sufficient foothold or a position of sufficient authority, the command from the Soviet capital may call for the demobilization of the armies of these nations or for their general demilitarization. A somewhat more elaborate procedure may consist in a declaration that these other countries are incapable of defending their neutrality, present or future, in the event of war, and to see that this is properly attended to, with the added request that Soviet troops be permitted to enter certain areas, or that certain military or naval bases be turned over (or perhaps "leased") to the Soviet authorities—all possibly under an agreement of "mutual assistance."

More prompt and more expeditious, and more thoroughgoing action is to be had in charging the governments of the other countries with fomenting or permitting secret plans or activities hostile to the Soviet state, or with conniving or conspiring or contracting alliance with certain "capitalistic" or "imperialistic" nations, or with engaging in intrigues that run counter to the well-being of that state. In such case a new and stronger agreement may be insisted upon, perhaps with the bidding that there be installed a pro-Soviet government, the better to attend to the fulfillment of the mutual assistance pact, and with the admission of an increased number of Soviet soldiers. Now is the time for the organization or promotion of an effective local communist party, which is betimes to assume the reins of government. Next in order may be the release of loud cries of protest respecting the "horrible" or "intolerable" conditions prevailing among the working classes or peasants. A variation of the theme may be that friends of the Soviet land were undergoing mistreatment or persecution, or that the authorities were not cordial toward those who would cultivate closer ties with that land, or that attempts were being made to suppress agitators favoring such closer ties; in other words, the government of the other state was to desist from any efforts to check this fifth column within its borders. Strong representations were now to be expected from Moscow that relations with the Soviet state were imperiled by such actions. The Soviet state, it was solemnly proclaimed, was duty-bound to protect its friends, treacherous plotters though they were against their own state.

At this point the stage is set, the time is ripe, for the creation of a puppet Soviet government, and its being placed in the seat of power. The formality of an "election" is gone through—but with only one ticket in the field, with soldiers at the ballot places, with the voter required to produce official papers indicating his right to vote—and with only one result possible. Those who are "elected" immediately set up a movement for annexation with the U.S.S.R. Formal petition in the name of the peasants, workers, and soldiers is made to Moscow for union, the new state now to participate in the activities and share in the blessings of the Soviet order. Moscow does its part with all due solemnity in carrying out this mockery of free and democratic institutions. By it, and as was to be expected, the whole proceeding is loudly acclaimed as having practically unanimous popular endorsement.

After the absorption of the helpless victim of Soviet tyranny into its body, the initial step in introducing the new order is likely to be the nationalization of banks, industries, and the larger farms; small farms with a limited amount of live stock are for the time being left in the hands of individual owners or occupants, to await the complete nationalization of the country.

To make sure of the unanimity of the expression of the popular will, the most active or the most determined of the enemies of U.S.S.R. or those least inclined to see the light, are whisked away—are banished or otherwise disposed of. After the absorption of the ill-fated land into the Soviet state, the latter has the impudence, the gall, to declare that it has been greeted "with tears of joy, with delirious exultation, with speeches, flowers, songs." It can show pictures, it is true; but how could these helpless folk, if not a picked group, resist the orders for their display of jubilation?

All these things proceed with Moscow proclaiming, as is its wont, high ethical and humanitarian considerations and standards—applying in its international transactions no less than in its domestic ones, and all in the name of the one true democracy of the world. It is to be added that the Soviet state has little compunction in aligning itself to a greater or less extent, with militaristic dictator states as and when its interests are to be served—few qualms, when the occasion arises, in making common cause with the enemies of the democracies to the injury of the latter.

Once we thought that if Soviet communism were to gain possession of the world, it would be by propaganda, by direct appeal, by indoctrination among a sufficient portion

of the population of the country to be affected, when
enough persons had been made to see and approve the
Soviet way and the Soviet program. This process appar-
ently, as was the taking over of peasant farms by intellectual argument, has proved too slow. Now we have before
us the application of force, something already applied
within the land to recalcitrant elements, next to be applied
without as well—to lands whose people prefer their own
ways, including democratic processes. Not necessarily by
moral suasion any longer, but by brute force as may be
needed, Soviet Russia would win over adherents to its
creed—that is, in such lands as are not able to resist except by superior force. Peaceful assurances issuing from
Moscow now stand before us in their naked worthlessness;
and peoples that would rely upon them do so at their peril.

Marxian socialism was not to proceed after any such
fashion. U.S.S.R. has gone it one better. "Imperialism"
never appeared in a form more raw or more bald, even
though the Soviet state disclaims any such appellation.
Charging other nations with "imperialism" and with "imperialistic" designs, it would outdo them in imperialistic
pursuits. It has taken on a dark-hued imperialistic cast,
even while rendering fulsome lip homage to democratic
institutions. It cannot escape even though it may cynically
assert that what it does is in keeping with the spirit of the
times.

No land unless very strong may now feel itself secure
from Soviet physical action. Whatever its trumped-up,
self-exonerating pleas, it may without qualm or scruple
proceed to take over such territory and such populations
as it pleases or as suits its purposes, and as it is able, and
by sheer force—when it has gathered sufficient strength
to itself—whatever the high-sounding language that may
be used as to the need of protection of the working
classes in other countries or as to the designs of "capitalis-

tic" nations. It will not be slow in finding excuses for the "liberation" of oppressed peoples in lands not its own, who it alleges are clamoring to be taken in. It is these considerations that are to determine the rôle of Soviet Russia as a peace-abiding or as an aggressor state. In the event of a hard war, involving a heavy and weakening drain upon Soviet man power and physical resources, the position of the country in respect to other nations will be greatly affected.

The world may now see that U.S.S.R. is not altogether to be counted upon as an assurance or safeguard for peace. The Soviet state is not the "bulwark against war and aggression" that some of its fond and credulous admirers have declaimed. Instead of being a sort of guarantor or champion of the world's peace, as it announced itself, and as the world was inclined to believe, the world has cause for distrust of it in any such capacity. Its protestations of peace, if not to go for nought, are at least to be considerably discounted. Rather than as a bird of peace bearing an olive branch for the earth, Soviet Russia looms up as a bird of more somber hue threatening such peace as may be left to the world, and ready for its own ends to tear apart whatever loose threads of peace yet persist among us. Whatever dark counsels with respect to international matters may prevail in the Kremlin remain its own dark secret; its international policies are unpredictable.

CHAPTER XV

A FINAL REVIEW

THE SOCIALIST state, dreamed of, yearned for, and struggled after by great numbers among the sons of men, has after long years of parturition arrived among them—in the form presented in Soviet Russia. It is said there that the great experiment has worked well, but has not been completed—that the country is not yet ready for the transition from socialism to the final desired communism. Operations there are not as clear as we should like. Our vision of what has taken place is more or less dimmed or distorted; we have not been able to see as through a crystal clear glass. But we have perceived something of what has occurred. From the spirit and the methods alike there is much to be learned—some things to our advantage, some things by way of warning.

The experiment in the Soviet state has been a startling one. The world cannot easily get over its shock. No such experiment has ever been attempted in human society. The experiment here has been tried in a vast, unwieldy land, in very many ways the last place on this earth of ours for such an undertaking. Was the experiment in the wisest, fittest hands? Could it count upon balanced, unwarped powers of judgment in its leaders—considering the material they had to work upon?

How near the great experiment has come to success, or how far removed it has been from success, is a question for later years to answer. Possibly even the socialist might have to declare that after all it never got much beyond an embryonic state. Even at best it has shown few signs of approaching the classless order, the goal of the orthodox communist.

In Soviet Russia we find one of the two extremes possible in men's governing of themselves—the absolutist, or totalitarian, or complete state control—the farthest perhaps in this direction that they have ever gone. We may ask if the notion of collectivism among men has not been carried so far that there is no longer room for the conception of the individual man as such or of individual action on his part. Apart, moreover, from the matter of communism, we may also ask if there has not been effected too much organization here, if there is not overorganization and topheaviness thrust to such lengths as to make a state itself really less effective. Or does communism permit no alternative?

The world would be stupid if it failed to realize and appreciate certain quite notable achievements of the Soviet state, and if it failed to put to account whatever steps forward in human progress may have been brought to pass there. In more than one matter it may to its advantage take a leaf from the Soviet notebook. In more than one particular the Soviet experiment offers a challenge to the rest of the earth. If the Soviet order is found to be wanting, and the order prevailing elsewhere is to survive and to constitute the future pattern for man, the world will do well to give itself a heart-searching examination in the light of Soviet efforts, and to learn better therefrom what it lacks and how it may take measures for its improvement and reform. This remains true, however much we may disavow and repudiate communistic principles in general or their manifestation in the Soviet state.

We can admire the zeal of the Soviet state in the wide educational program being provided for its citizens, even though we do not regard its methods and aims as always the soundest, even though we feel that it must be purged of its political bearings, and even though we are struck with horror at making education a political thing. We can approve the importance given to technical education in respect to the conditions of modern life. We can express our gratification over the high place bestowed upon scientific research. We can appreciate the realization of the increasing amount of leisure time being made available to the people through technological advance and the importance of making some provision for it. We can commend the attitude displayed toward backward peoples and peoples hitherto denied so much of human rights, with whatever advance toward the brotherhood of man is signified here. We can think well of the simplicity and frugality of those who hold office in the land, and of the spirit of a land that does not regard the possession of great wealth as the best measure of success. We can applaud the efforts to have a people physically hearty and sound, and as far as possible free from illness. We can view without disfavor humanitarian conceptions introduced into various phases of public service. We can say a good word for the encouragement of coöperative attitudes among the people in the doing of their tasks and in the building up of the country. We can extend praise for the insistent demand for the maximum production of goods in the land, including the utmost development of natural resources, so that as many as possible may enjoy the satisfactions of life. We can offer our benediction for the dignity that is at least theoretically given to labor in the organization of human society, even though we may doubt if labor in its practical bearings has fared altogether well in the Soviet land. We cannot be without gratitude that there has been called to the attention of men a possible social order where the wealth created should be more widely and equitably shared.

But we cannot refrain from asking at the same time if these things might not have been approached in circumstances that would have held in honor the finer values of human existence, such as have been cherished by man as essential to his real progress, and in circumstances that would not have done violence to his spirit.

However much we may appreciate what the people of Russia have gone through in years past, and can realize the truth of the ancient saying that where the wind is sown, there will the whirlwind be reaped; however much we can understand how a people so grievously and cruelly downtrodden would in due time be moved to secure the just rights of men; and however much we can comprehend natural efforts toward a better political, economic, and social order—yet notwithstanding all this, mankind has been appalled and aghast at the excesses that have taken place in Russia in the name of these things. Even if that country were found to have made notable advance or to have attained a measure of success in her political, economic, and social undertakings, we would be constrained to cry: At what price this advance or success!

How many unhappy peasant proprietors have been uprooted from simple homes, driven to freezing Arctic climates, maltreated and tortured, perhaps even paying with their lives—for nothing but a love for their little farms which they wished to cultivate themselves, and the fruits of which they wished to enjoy for themselves and their families, or because they possessed too many cows or horses, or cultivated their land a bit too thriftily? How many citizens have been compelled to toil at forced labor, with insufficient food, hounded and beaten by secret police, or herded into wretched concentration camps, perhaps stood before a firing squad—for nothing more heinous than some infraction of a meticulous, sumptuary, arbitrary code or government behest, perhaps mere disagree-

ment with government authorities, or as an object lesson
for those who might think of disagreeing too far or of re-
sisting at all—perhaps for lack of sufficient enthusiasm in
certain government projects? What has been the extent
of the periodic blood purges—of own party members of
government officialism, often of those in positions of influence and authority in those earliest Soviet days, often of
the ablest and most intelligent, perhaps with the best
brains of the nation? Can it be that in the new Russia
political prisoners are subjected to greater hardship and
cruelty than in the old; that there are more mass killings
now than then? Can it be that we are to have in these
respects something, not better but worse, than what we
knew of the Russia of the Czars, which was said to be an
absolutism tempered with assassination—ruthless violence from above countered with ruthless violence from
below?

What is to be said of a land that to carry on a determined, doctrinaire economic and political policy has to
fly in the face of so much that has proved good for the
human race? What is to be said of a land that in the name
of communism boldly and frankly repudiates the hard-
won conceptions of democracy, and sets up a dictatorship
of power and force in the hands of the few for the governing of the many, not even rendering lip service to the principle that all governments derive their just powers from
the consent of the governed, or that the individual citizen
has certain rights deserving of respect, even from government? What is to be said of a land that has so little
esteem for human personality, for the dignity of human
beings that it will betray its own citizens and ruthlessly
crush them beneath? What is to be said of a land where
upon literature, art, science is exercised more or less undisguised coercion? What is to be said of a land that, to
carry out a particular economic or political program, has

to resort to the cold-blooded wrenching of the human race from its high place in the things of the spirit? What is to be said of a land that under the guise of recreating its institutions and of building up a new social order, of purely materialistic character, on purely materialistic foundations, and with purely materialistic outlook, seeks to trample under foot much of the finer flowers of civilization—so much of what man has found noble in human living? What is to be said of a land indoctrinated with a philosophy that in respect to the rights and concerns of others is hard, narrow, soulless, jaundiced, illiberal, dogmatic, fanatical, bigoted—a philosophy that has no qualms or scruples as to the end justifying the means, whatever the fair-spoken and high-sounding phrase or whatever the moving slogan employed, or however much in the means there may be involved of violence, of oppression, of cruelty? What is to be said of a land, once overconfidently believed to offer an assurance of world peace, now throwing off more or less of its disguise and ready to make war simply to force its way of life upon weaker nations, and quite against their will, to dispossess and enslave—an "imperialism" raw and unblushing? What is to be said of a land calling itself a true democracy, that plays fast and loose with the enemies of democracy?

Is there not something about the whole Soviet undertaking that rings hollow, something that is mechanical, that goes against the highest aspirations of the human spirit? Is there not in it something made of iron, into which the freedom of man can never be moulded, can never be fitted? Is there not something brought into being that is stifling to what is cherished in man's heart, something by which is smothered his truest being? Is there not something that wars against the very soul of man?

Men of intelligence and with humanity of heart must reject the doctrine that the play of economic forces, however tremendous it is after all, is the sole or the main determining factor in human conduct, and that nothing else need be reckoned with. Such doctrine can only shrivel if not destroy the soul of man. That, furthermore, the evils of the world can be traced or attributed to a particular economic order, and that with its ending and the substitution of another all will be well, is something hardly to be accepted. Nor can we look with favor upon the conception—no matter what the brave language used to establish it—of a "mass-man," so far "socialized" that he no longer has an individual personality, worthy of respect and regard, and without the qualities and aspirations to which man is everlastingly the heir.

However vast the evils in human affairs, whatever their depth, and whatever their breadth, is it not possible to remove them and thus to effect a better state for men, to separate the good from the bad and to concentrate our attacks upon the latter—without indiscriminate destruction, and without the creation of new evils to exist side by side with whatever has been achieved?

In the Soviet land there is not given a large place in the vocabulary to such old-fashioned things as character or principle or honor or integrity, and seemingly little more in its general conceptions—at least little beyond what may be involved in allegiance to this despotic state. And here as well as elsewhere it may be found sometimes that chickens have a way of coming home to roost. It is doubtful if very many of the apologists for and panegyrists of the Soviet state who live in other lands would willingly choose to make this their permanent home. For somehow with respect to this land men have not come to large faith. There is distrust within, without.

The state should somehow forever remain the servant of man; it should not emerge with such strength in its hands as to become a Frankenstein and make men cower before it. And when a state is not implanted upon democracy, but is antagonistic thereto, there is multiplied peril alike to man and to his advance.

The Soviet state calls itself a liberating power for the spirit of man. Is it not rather a power for the defeat, for the subjugation of that spirit? Will that spirit accept, save at the cost of its own repudiation?

Socialism, so far as it is an economic doctrine, and as such entitled to a respectful hearing among the possible programs offered for man's economic well-being, has nothing to do with all such unholy attitudes. If socialism means greater reliance and greater insistence upon the conception of human brotherhood, this is all the more reason why the spiritual values of life should not be dragged down and trampled in the dust. Perhaps Soviet Russia with its experiments on so gigantic and so moving a scale will have given to mankind an awesome lesson— one that should stand it in good stead for long years to come.

Perhaps, however, the outstanding tragedy of the matter is that because of the peculiar temperament of the Soviet state, with its low ratings upon certain old-fashioned principles, upon elemental moral foundations, upon conceptions stressing the need of a house being built upon a rock—considerations that man after all cannot get along without, whether in a socialist or in a non-socialist state —we are not in a position to determine whether state socialism has had a fair trial in the Union of Socialist Soviet Republics, or has been or could have been successful there, or has there made distinctly helpful contributions in solving the economic, political, and social problems of man's world.